A-FARMING WE W

Born in 1916 during the First World War, Sonia spent her childhood at a succession of boarding schools and with governesses, seeing little of her parents. Her first book, *Making The Most Of It*, tells of these early years and how she joined the Women's Auxiliary Air Force at the start of the Second World War – and learned how to make the most of the opportunities the W.A.A.F. gave her. This second volume of her memoirs continues her story in the years after the war.

Sonia wrote her books between 1986 and 1996 after being encouraged to write down as many as possible of the stories she often told to her family and friends. A creative writing course encouraged her to use her natural talent for witty narrative and memory for detail. Domestic circumstances prevented her from publishing at the time, but later her manuscripts were rediscovered and have at last been brought to the world at large.

ALSO IN BRIERLEY BOOKS
BY SONIA TUDOR

Making The Most Of It

A-Farming We Will Go
From Hong Kong to Herefordshire

Sonia Tudor

Brierley Books

Published by Brierley Books
www.brierleybooks.co.uk

Copyright © Sonia Tudor 2011
All rights reserved. No part of this publication may be reproduced in any material form whether by photocopying or storing in any medium by electronic means (whether or not transiently or incidentally to some other use of this publication) without the prior written consent of the copyright owner except in accordance with the provisions of the Copyright, Designs and Patents Act 1988. Applications for the copyright owner's written permission to reproduce any part of this publication should be addressed to the Publisher.

Sonia Tudor has asserted her moral right to be identified as the author of this book.

Photographs (except where otherwise stated) by Henry Tudor, Sonia Tudor, Guy Sawrey-Cookson and Lady Eva Tudor.
Paintings by Lady Eva Tudor
Cover by Lady Eva Tudor: Caldicott Farm

WARNING: The doing of any unauthorised act in relation to this work may result in both civil and criminal liability.
No responsibility for the loss occasioned to any person acting or refraining from acting as a result of the material contained in this publication will be accepted by the authors or publishers.

ISBN 978-0-9566396-1-5
Printed by CLE Print Ltd.
First edition 2011

In Memory of Harry, with whom I had the Happiest Times of My Life

A-Farming We Will Go
From Hong Kong to Herefordshire

Sonia Tudor

Introduction

In my last book, *Making The Most Of It*, I wrote about my early days, going through a succession of boarding schools and governesses and then finding myself as a Code and Cypher W.A.A.F. officer in World War II, having adventures and escapades in Italy, Egypt, Algiers and sundry places *en route*. Just as I was returning to England I came across Wing Commander Harry Tudor, who looked after me in the last few days in Italy and on board ship back to England. By the time we had returned to our respective bases we were engaged. Not long after, although it was still wartime, we married and settled in the air force base at Earls Colne. By September 1945 we were both demobilised and living in a house not far away, in Jasper's Green near Braintree. That is where this book begins.

8

One
Hong Kong

It happened rather quickly just before Christmas.

After the war in 1945 we were living temporarily in a little cottage called King's Croft in Jasper's Green. My husband Harry had been in the Hong Kong and Shanghai Bank before the war and he intended to continue his career with them, so we were waiting for him to be sent back to Hong Kong. In December we had the call. Harry and I went up to London and spent the night with friends. The next day Harry took off for Hong Kong by air. He left in a flying boat from England and then flew over various bits of water as far as the northern part of India, where he landed on a lake and then proceeded by very small hops to Hong Kong. I was very relieved that he arrived safely.

We had paid for a further three months rent on King's Croft, but I was lonely, so I invited one of my ex-wartime friends to stay. She was married and widowed during the war and was living with her in-laws and her little son by the sea nearby.

After the lease expired I most reluctantly went to live with my mother-in-law, Lady Tudor, in a large, cold, old, decrepit house near Bury St. Edmunds.

I managed to escape several times to stay with friends and relations not too far away, all the time awaiting my summons to go to Hong Kong. Eventually it happened. While I was staying with Maxie in Dublin in June 1946, a telegram arrived from the Colonial Office in London. A passage had been arranged for me on the S.S. Otranto. So I rushed back to Bury St. Edmunds effervescent with excitement.

A cable had just arrived there for me from Harry. It said, "ACCOMMODATION ARRANGED SEE YOU SOON." This was good news. The bank had decreed that wives could travel out to Hong Kong as soon as the Colonial Office provided a passage, but only if their spouses had found somewhere for them to live. Normally the bank would have had some form of married quarters for couples like us, but these houses and flats had been wrecked by the Japanese soldiers.

The Otranto, the ship on which I was to make the long journey, was the sister ship to the S.S. Orcades on which I had sailed four years earlier from England to Durban.

A small flock of meek, well-behaved Hong Kong Bank wives embarked at Tilbury. The Otranto was still equipped as a troop-ship, so I found myself very much at home. It was just like wartime days to be sharing a double cabin with seven other women. However, this time there was to be no coming to bed late. No climbing up to the top bunk in the dark, often standing on the face of the occupant of the lower bunk. No more pulsating shipboard romances. No more rendezvous on the boat deck in the moonlight. On this voyage every Hong Kong Bank wife had to behave impeccably.

Amongst the other passengers were a group of younger Hong Kong bankers destined to join the Junior Mess on the top of the Peak. This party had all served in the Forces and, although some were not yet twenty-eight, many had ignored the bank's rules and married.

John Muriel, a reliable 'thirty-something' bachelor, took charge of them and also of the 'Wives'. I shared a table with a Mrs. Jock Dunneth, a Mrs. Max Haymes and a Mrs. Philip Sellars, otherwise known as Marion, Betty and Frédérique. Our table was presided over by a pleasant, middle-aged ship's officer. He too kept a watchful eye on us and if we went ashore, we were literally shepherded around by either of these two.

Another link with the past was the head barman. He greeted me like an old friend saying, with a cheerful leer, that he remembered me on the Orcades on which he had also been head barman. I was glad to see him again if only because the Orcades had been torpedoed and sunk on its return journey to England from Durban. We had heard that many people on board had drowned and only a few had survived.

Colombo was one of the ports where the wives went ashore and sat on the verandah of the Galle Face Hotel sipping drinks. A few days later *en route* for the next stop, Singapore, I started to feel ill. The ship's doctor told me I had some kind of fever. He did not know exactly what, but we might as well call it 'Colombo Fever'. I was to stay in my bunk until my temperature dropped. So I only glimpsed Singapore out of a porthole. The other wives enjoyed the hottest curry of their lives in the Hong Kong Bank Mess, followed by a soothing pudding called *Gula Melaka*. This was made, they told me, of tapioca. Afterwards they had visited Raffles Hotel. Lucky things!

After Singapore our final stop would be Hong Kong and I was determined to be fit again by then. But I did not know that while I had been confined to bunk, in Hong Kong Harry was having yet another bout of malaria and was much more ill than I had been.

We sailed into Hong Kong harbour on a clear sunny morning. I saw for the first time the skyscraper-dominated skyline of the island south of the harbour, and the lower and less impressive Kowloon side with the open country of the New Territories on the horizon. The harbour itself seemed almost completely covered with shipping, ranging from liners, naval craft of various sizes and ferryboats to Chinese junks and sampans. Whole families of people including their livestock - ducks, hens, goats, cats, dogs and even the occasional pig - lived together in harmony on the larger junks.

At last the Otranto tied up and, leaning over the rails, I spotted among the crowd two stick-insect-like persons gazing up at us. I recognised Harry and the other person proved to be Max Haymes, Betty's husband, who had, like Harry, just recovered from malaria.

During the six-week journey there had been much speculation amongst the wives about exactly what 'accommodation' was awaiting them. After a joyous reunion, Harry put me into the Baby Austin which we had shipped out some months previously and said mysteriously that he was now taking us to our new, though temporary, home. One room in a large block somewhere in downtown Victoria, I guessed.

But the car started to ascend the Peak, zig-zagging its way up and round the mountain. At the top, far above the upper limit of the Peak Tram, Harry drove onto a road encircling the very summit of the small mountain. This was Mount Kellett Road. He turned into a drive on the right and stopped outside an imposing house.

"You have kept on asking me what the 'accommodation' is that I have found for us. Well, this is it!" he said.

I could not believe my eyes. This was neither one room nor a very small flat but instead a magnificent dwelling with a garden and a wonderful view down to the sea and a little fishing village with the unexpected name of Aberdeen.

"Is *all* this just for us?" I asked.

"Not quite," said Harry, "We're sharing it for three or four months with a man called Arthur Potter. He is the Chief Education Officer in the Colony.

The name of this Shangri-La was 'Erewhon'. The reason it had not been wrecked like nearly all the other houses on the Peak was because a Japanese doctor had decided to live in it. Inside it was spacious and cool and I met our fellow tenant, Arthur Potter, a jolly, little man with one wooden leg. Just the job, he assured me, for walking about on the sides of mountains.

There were five other occupants of 'Erewhon'. In order of precedence they were: Cheng Yau, the cook-boy, though in reality no 'boy'. He was elderly, with the skin stretched so tightly across his face and eyebrows raised so high that he looked perpetually surprised. He was completely clad in dazzling white.

Second was his wife known only as Wash Amah. We never knew her real name. She too wore white.

Third was the coolie, their nephew Chun. He always wore black.

And the remaining two in the package deal were a little boy and a girl called Pun and Yin. Their mother had been Cheng Yau and the Wash Amah's daughter. She had been killed by the Japanese, so their grandparents were bringing them up. Their father, whom we saw occasionally, worked on a ship.

Cheng Yau did the cooking and shopping. Chun did the housework. The Wash Amah did everybody's washing - all by hand.

The only reason we could live in such luxury on the Peak was because we had the little car. All provisions for eight people had to be fetched from downtown Victoria. Cheng Yau would set out daily in the afternoon, descending in the Peak Tram which was about ten minutes' walk away. But he could not carry all his purchases far: they were much too heavy and his load usually included a large lump of ice wrapped in sacking. There was no fridge at 'Erewhon'. So he would position himself and all his shopping outside the Hong Kong Bank building at 5 p.m. and Harry would transport him home.

Nowadays, I am told, the top of the Peak is covered with new houses. Then, in 1946, there were very few buildings left standing. One of these was the empty former Naval Hospital. There was also one block of flats, the Hong Kong Bank's Junior Mess, and, of course, 'Erewhon' (Nowhere, spelt backwards).

The house on the Peak, 'Erewhon'

Sonia in the house on the Peak

When Harry departed each morning for work, he left me in a beautiful Garden of Eden, containing, so I thought, no other living soul apart from the Cheng Yau family and the servants at the Peak Mess. On clear, sunny days this was blissful, and I could explore the surrounding roads, the ruined houses and their gardens and walk about amongst the lush vegetation on the slopes of the Peak. There were numerous flowering shrubs I had never seen before, including lantana (which though so colourful, unfortunately smelled of tomcat). The area was full of exotic birds, many of them species of bulbul. One of these had been given the name of the 'Come-to-the-Peak-Ha-Ha' bird, for that was what it appeared to be saying.

But sometimes the top of the Peak, nearly two thousand feet high, was covered with cloud. 'Visibility - Birds Walking', as the R.A.F. used to say. Then it was very lonely, as well as a very damp place too. I discovered why every house at that height had to have one large, permanently heated room where all linen and everybody's clothes had to be kept. Otherwise these clothes and linen swiftly became mouldy and mildewed. On days like that I would grope my way down to the top of the Peak Tram and descend to the humid, bustling atmosphere of Victoria, where all my shipboard friends lived.

But I was wrong about being the only person in my private Garden of Eden. There were already two resident Serpents who soon made themselves known to me. They took the form of the Colonial Judge and his sidekick the Legal Advisor. The two men lived together in that one surviving block of flats. Often when I was roaming about happily exploring the Peak these two pests would suddenly materialise. They were both in their fifties and unfortunately their wives had not yet arrived from England. Also unfortunately for me I was for them 'Hobson's Choice'. When we met they would ogle me unashamedly and make embarrassing personal remarks. Then they would try to entice me back to their lair for 'a little drink, or at least a cup of coffee'. I always refused, though extremely politely.

Why were they wandering about on the Peak during working hours, I wondered. Why were they not down in Victoria 'judging' or 'legally advising'?

I told Harry about the unsavoury duo, who we unfortunately also met occasionally on social occasions, and often on a swimming beach. We decided to call the Judge the D.O.M. - Dirty Old Man - and the Legal Advisor the V.D.O.M. - Very Dirty Old Man. I longed to bang their two stupid heads together, but it would not do to antagonise these two comparatively important people. Harry and I might then find ourselves summarily posted to Borneo, Papua New Guinea or some other unappetising place where the Hong Kong Bank had a branch.

My problem with the D.O.M. and the V.D.O.M. did not last long. After three months of living on the Peak we descended, literally, to the flat. This was across the harbour to Kowloon. Kowloon then, if not now, was definitely downmarket. All the 'best' people lived on the Island. But this did not bother us. Five or six identical three-storey houses had been bought and refurbished by the bank in Waterloo Road. Outwardly they were ugly, built of grey concrete and each with a garage, but without a vestige of garden or any greenery at all.

Inside, to me anyhow, they seemed the height of luxury. Each flat 'afforded' or 'comprised of' in Estate Agent Speak, two commodious bedrooms, two bathrooms, dining room, sitting room, large square covered verandah, modern kitchen and 'adequate' servants' quarters. In our case, Cheng Yau, Wash Amah and Chun plus the children, Pun and Yin, had to fit into five very small rooms. Their kitchen had an open charcoal fire. Their ablutions were adequate though basic, and five people had to squeeze into the three other little cells. But that small extended family, like us, seemed very satisfied with their lot.

Harry caught the Star Ferry each morning to cross to the Island to work; and I was happy to find one of my best friends living in a flat next door. Our lives were very different now from our previous existences in England. All kinds of goods were being imported into the Colony, mostly from the U.S.A.. No coupons were needed for food or clothes. Suits and dresses could be made to measure overnight, almost 'while-you-wait'. The 'Dairy Farm' on Hong Kong Island was *the* place to visit for coffee and luscious cream cakes, and fresh milk from genuine cows could be bought there. Tennis and swimming plus more coffee and cakes took place at the United Services Club in Kowloon. Bank staff and their families were allowed to be members. We rapidly grew fat.

Chinese millionaires, helped in their businesses by the bank, sometimes invited bank families to enormous Chinese dinner parties. My memory of these occasions is hazy, because the only drink served with the food was champagne and the room was always very hot. After many preceding courses the 'Flat Ducks' would be brought in. I had seen these strange birds festooned round Chinese butchers' shops. They looked as if they had been plucked and drawn and then run over by a steamroller. Now they reappeared cooked, their plumpness restored, and arranged so cleverly that they seemed whole. In reality they had already been carved into suitably sized portions. Harry who had had many years' experience of using chopsticks was very adept. I was hopeless and would have gone very hungry if some kind and thoughtful person had not eventually handed me a spoon and fork.

At Christmas expensive presents were sent by the same millionaires to bank staff they had found helpful: at our first Christmas Harry was given a packing-case full of stem ginger in beautiful jars. He did not like ginger. Luckily, I did. When the next Christmas came round I was still munching my way through the previous year's present. That Christmas Harry was given a crate of whisky. It suited him much better.

By this time some of the female lotus-eaters were beginning to feel a bit jaded by the combination of too much rich food, too much drink, too much leisure and no useful work to do. All the usual household tasks were forbidden to us.

In the Tudor flat Cheng Yau was omnipotent. I realised that:

No housework was allowed. Chun did that.

No bed-making. Cheng Yau did that.

No washing. Wash Amah did that.

No washing up either and certainly *No* cooking.

And those wives who had children had to hand them over to the Baby Amah who took complete charge.

Each day Cheng Yau would have an audience with me, armed with notebook and pencil. In theory, together we would concoct a shopping list for him to take to market. In practice he put all the words into my mouth. He wrote his list in writing and language *he* could understand. I wrote my list more or less at his dictation.

The ceremony invariably started with Cheng Yau saying, "We need ve-apolated milk, Missy".

"Yes, Cheng Yau, we do need evaporated milk," I would agree.

Then we would each write down items like 'Bean Spros' (bean sprouts to me), 'flesh eggs', 'lice' and all the other weird things Cheng Yau thought necessary.

But at the end I always had to prompt him. "Don't forget vegetables, Cheng Yau".

"No Missy, I no forget veshibibubbles," he would reply. This word defeated him and trying to say it made him spit.

Cheng Yau was a keen cook, and soon after I arrived in Hong Kong a birthday came round. Harry suggested that Cheng Yau should make a birthday cake and write 'Happy Birthday' on top. Cheng Yau, full of enthusiasm, went ahead and made a most magnificent chocolate birthday cake. Unfortunately, he could not spell well and did not speak good English. What he had written so carefully was 'Happy Bathday'.

He was delighted when Harry took lots of photographs of him holding this cake: a very happy occasion.

With two friends I approached the lady who seemed to organise every kind of Social Service in the Colony: the wife of the Medical Officer of Health Dr. O'Ryan. Mrs. O'Ryan herself was a 'White Russian'. I had never met one before and often wondered why they were called White Russians. The obvious but probably incorrect answer was as a contrast to the Reds who had taken over Russia after the 1917 Revolution. Then the whites, the aristocratic and upper classes, had fled, many to Paris and some to places like Shanghai. This is where Dr. O'Ryan had found his super-efficient and at times overpowering wife.

"Yes," said the great lady, she could find a useful little job for us. In contrast to the immensely rich Chinese businessmen, there was a great deal of poverty and malnourishment among the lowest classes. She suggested we helped to hand out tins of condensed milk to deserving babies in Wan Chai, a very poor district of Victoria.

It sounded an extremely simple though useful job. We sat behind a trestle table in a godown in Wan Chai, next to a small mountain of crates containing tins of condensed milk. The babies came, mostly in their mothers' arms, or sometimes carried on the backs of small but older brothers and sisters.

We thought the task was well within the capabilities of three 'idle-rich' women.

But the following week Mrs. O'Ryan arrived to inspect us at work, bringing with her a tin opener, the old-fashioned, simple kind used to jab the tops of tins. Wan Chai Market had been flooded with tins of condensed milk after our duties last week, she said. The local mothers preferred to sell the milk rather than pour it into their babies. This week we were to stab the lid of each tin before handing it over. So one of us stabbed, the second handed, and the third received and counted the now sticky as well as smelly paper money.

Sonia, Harry and Cheng Yau's grandchildren, Pun and Yin

Cheng Yau and the 'bathday' cake

The following week Mrs. O'Ryan appeared again and her eagle eye noted another fault on our part.

"Stop the milk distribution!" she cried, "Have none of you noticed that the same baby is coming back several times for another tin of milk?"

All Chinese babies looked very similar to us, but it was true. One baby would appear firstly in its mother's arms, then return later on its little brother's back and yet again with a different carrier. From now on, we were told, each baby had to be ink-stamped on the back of its left hand before the milk was handed over.

At last we got the hang of this simple task and it continued for many months.

Harry and I looked forward to each weekend. On Saturday morning a Cantonese gentleman arrived to give him a two-hour Cantonese lesson. After that we were free to go off to explore the open country of the New Territories. Only a few of our bank friends did this. For some strange reason it was 'not done'. It was easy to get into this unknown terrain. All we had to do was walk to the end of Waterloo Road, where the tarmac terminated in front of what was called the Lion Rock: in reality a quite low, but very steep hill covered with grass and boulders. Once on the top we were in a different world. The New Territories were made up of farmland - mainly rice paddies and pasture for water buffaloes - lonely, secluded beaches and shrubby country with single-file paths leading to fishing villages and patches of jungle-type woodland. The only dangers were the occasional bad-tempered water buffalo or poisonous snake, and robbers.

On Sundays we could go further afield. Chun was put in the dicky seat of the Austin and we drove into the centre of the territory, parked the car and left it with Chun in charge. His job was to defend the Austin from what he and Cheng Yau called 'pilots'. At first we did not understand what they meant when they told us about pilots holding up

The view from the apartment

Harry in the Austin saloon

the train from Kowloon to the Chinese border and robbing all the passengers. Or why pilots should be so busy breaking into houses and flats in Victoria and Kowloon. Then we realised they were trying to say "pirates", an umbrella term for all kinds of wrongdoers. Poor Chun, a slight, timid youth, was terrified when left alone in charge of the car. He soon decided he would be safer at sea. So he left and Chen Yau produced another of his 'nephews' as a replacement.

Ah Wing could not have been more different. He was the nearest human being I have ever seen to a gorilla. His burly, square frame was dressed in grey Chinese garb, but his head was large, his forehead low, his nostrils wide, his eyebrows bristly and his hair short and stubby. In character he was gentle and kind. Luckily Ah Wing was not afraid of 'pilots' when left alone in the wilderness.

About this time we acquired a new car, sent out from England: again an Austin, but this time a saloon model and black in colour. All new cars after the end of the war were inevitably black for several years. The Baby Austin was sold immediately to a friend of Harry's, a very fat man called Colonel Bob Laming. They had known each other pre-war in Bangkok, and during the war Bob had been captured by the Japanese and forced to work on the infamous Burma-Siam railway. During this horrendous experience Bob had become very thin. But now he was restored to his usual rotund self. We would spot the little Austin careering around the streets of Kowloon and Victoria and turning corners on two wheels. Bob's weight needed a counterbalance. We had no need to worry, he assured us: his wife weighed as much as he did and would soon be joining him.

Out of boredom I joined the Scottish dancing classes held weekly in a humid hall in Victoria. We were of mixed nationalities, more females than males, but we did have one thing in common: our compulsory genuine black leather, lace-up-the-leg, flat-soled, Scottish dancing shoes. When our instructor thought we were sufficiently proficient, he organised a Highland Ball at the Hong Kong Hotel. We were all to bring a partner. I asked Harry if he could do Scottish Dancing? "Of course," he replied.

It was a dinner dance, and after a large meal the Scottish Dancing began. We were told to come onto the dance floor. Harry came with me, but when the music began for 'The Dashing White Sergeant' he did not join the rest. Instead he performed a solo 'Sailor's Hornpipe' in the middle of the floor. That was the only Scottish dance he knew, he said.

One of the reasons Harry had weekly lessons in Cantonese was because he believed if you lived in a foreign country, you ought to be able to speak the language and converse with the inhabitants. He had already learnt some Cantonese during his first stay in Hong Kong and then when sent to Bangkok had learnt to speak Thai. This was now a bit confusing for him because Cantonese and Thai are both tonal languages. The same syllables spoken in several different tones can have as many different meanings. Now, as well, he was getting mixed up with the two very similar languages.

For practice he talked to any Cantonese person he met while we were exploring the countryside at weekends. They were both delighted and surprised to be addressed in their own language by this Englishman: few others bothered to learn. One day on a prowl round the more rural outskirts of Kowloon, we were in an area of small market gardens where most of the colony's vegetables were grown. There we met a tall, young Chinese man with artistic-looking hair, and his girlfriend. Harry started talking to him and they got on famously. The girlfriend and I felt quite left out: neither of us were linguists, so we could only smile at each other. When Harry asked the young man what he did for a living, he replied proudly in English, "I am Poet". Their conversation continued for quite a while and when we eventually parted company, Harry told me we had been invited to visit them in their flat in 'Leydon Load'.

"Where is Leydon Load?" I asked.

"I think he means Nathan Road," Harry told me.

On the day arranged we were given a polite and smiley welcome by the Poet and his girlfriend and shown into the sitting room. This at first seemed rather gloomy. The colour scheme was unrelieved brown, with ornately and uncomfortably carved, dark brown chairs without cushions, small, dark brown carved tables, a few ornaments and two vast, dark brown spittoons to match. We were served with bitter green tea, although I would have preferred dark brown, and very small, sweet, dark brown cakes. The Poet and Harry were soon having an animated conversation. The girlfriend and I smiled at each other and laughed heartily whenever the two men did. I knew very few words of Cantonese. One of these was 'Ho!' which means good. I could also say 'Ho! Ho!' which means very good, or even on occasion, 'Ho! Ho-a!' which means excellent, wonderful or superb. Every now and then I interjected a 'Ho!', 'Ho! Ho!', or 'Ho! Ho-a!' to show how interested I was.

When we left Harry said, "I have asked them to visit us next Saturday. We will give them drinks and 'small chow'. Cheng Yau will have to go out and buy some spittoons."

Cheng Yau was aghast when told two young Cantonese people had been invited for drinks. And when Harry told him he must buy two large spittoons, his eyebrows almost disappeared off the top of his head.

"Spiddoons? Master? You want *me* go buy spiddoons?"

"Yes please, Cheng Yau," Harry replied.

Cheng Yau left the room muttering to himself, obviously greatly shocked.

When the young couple came, they drank the drinks offered, obviously enjoyed Cheng Yau's 'small chow', a selection of mouthfuls of mainly hot cheesy things, made use of the spittoons and never missed once.

During our years together in Hong Kong there were many unforgettable first time experiences for me, if not for Harry. He was by this time almost an 'old China hand'.

So my first typhoon will always be remembered. Typhoon was the local Far Eastern name for a hurricane, though without a friendly human Christian name. When a typhoon was imminent, warnings were broadcast and its probable route announced. We heard the first warning during the early afternoon. Philip and Frédérique Sellars had invited us to a meal with them that evening. Philip was senior to Harry and the Sellars had been very lucky and been allotted the penthouse flat on top of the Hong Kong Bank building. Harry reckoned it would be quite safe to cross the harbour in the Star Ferry. The typhoon did not seem to be moving very fast.

At that time Frédérique was in an extreme state of excitement about her brother Jacques. He was a great friend and follower of the famous French Jazz quintet called *La Quintette Du Hot Club De France*. Two of its members were Stéphane Grappelli and Django Rheinhart. Frédérique already owned and played incessantly all the records made by the quintet. And now her brother had written and published a book about the band called *Le Jaz Hot*. The book had just arrived in Hong Kong. She was very keen for us to see and hear them.

A lift took us to the top of the tall building and to the Sellars' very comfortable flat. The *Hot Club* records, played non-stop at full volume, formed a noisy background to the whole evening. We did not hear the wind growing ever more tempestuous, nor the torrential rain outside. I did notice the top of the skyscraper was swaying a bit, but put that down to Philip continually filling my glass. After listening to the records while eating, we danced to them, each stomping around in our own version of the Charleston. Then, exhausted, we sat down while Frédérique in a loud voice declaimed passages from her brother's book. All the time Philip continued to re-fill our glasses. When he announced that the typhoon was almost overhead and that Harry and I must sleep

26

in their spare room, we were beyond caring or noticing what was going on in the world outside.

By the time we woke the next morning, the typhoon had passed and the ferry was once more running. Harry went straight to work, down below, and I returned to Kowloon, noticing on the way the fallen trees, abandoned cars and, sadly, the capsized sampans in the water.

In due course it was our turn to host a Sunday party on the *Wayfoong*, the Hong Kong Bank launch. Cheng Yau was in charge of the food and drink arrangements and we invited all our best friends. While the launch chugged sedately round the many little islands, some of our guests were towed in turn on surf boards. I tried this with Harry because I was quite incapable of standing up on my own. It was exhilarating until we fell off, when, while waiting for the launch to turn round and arrive to pick us up, I remembered the sharks. There were not many of these in the waters around Hong Kong ... or so they said. But people, mainly soldiers, who swam off Stanley Bay sometimes did not return at all, or else struggled minus a leg or arm. Another amusement on board was fishing. All kinds of unusual creatures were landed, and my first catch was a furious-looking fish, which immediately inflated itself on the deck and then bounced about like a football.

"No good eat," said Cheng Yau, tossing it back into the sea.

My next prize expressed its fury by emitting a spray of black, ink-like liquid.

"Velly good chow: now black gone, I take home," said Cheng Yau. We hoped we would not have to eat it.

During those years I had grown very fond of the two children Pun and Yin, especially Yin, the little girl. They did not go to school and seemed to lead a rather dull life with their grandparents. So, from time to time, we would take them with us when we went to explore an unknown beach in the New Territories. We had bought them bathing trunks and

On the H.S.B.C. motor launch, *Wayfoong*

Water-skiing on boards behind the *Wayfoong*

a bucket and spade each and although neither could swim they loved digging, paddling and splashing about.

One day, accompanied by Pun and Yin, we tried out another unfamiliar beach and as usual were the only people on it. Harry, with perhaps a hint of showing off, sprinted into the sea and flung himself backwards into the waves. He surfaced immediately, screaming with pain, and sprinted back up the beach just as fast. His back and chest looked as if they had been lashed with a cat-o'-nine-tails. Poor Harry had dived into a Portuguese Man of War, a huge jellyfish with a particularly nasty sting. With great haste we all dressed again, got into the car and drove swiftly to the first chemist shop in Kowloon. The Chinese owner was very sympathetic and knew exactly what should be done. He told Harry to go home, fill a bath with lukewarm water and after adding a large quantity of bicarbonate of soda, which he sold us, lie in the water for two hours. Harry followed these instructions to the letter and gradually the horrible red wheals and the pain subsided, although he bore the long marks of the stinging tentacles for many weeks.

It may sound as if those few years in Hong Kong were devoted entirely to lotus-eating. In some ways they were, although I gradually became bored with this life of comparative luxury with no useful job to do. It was like eating too many cream cakes with not enough plain bread and butter in between. A fascinating experience, but not a way of life forever.

As for Harry, he enjoyed his life with the bank, when he was not actually working in it. 'Square peg' Harry had known for years that he did not fit into the 'round hole' of a merchant banker. And in his case there was a fly in the ointment, or more accurately a mosquito, causing bouts of malaria. Far too often he was laid low with new attacks.

The bank doctor told him his only chance of defeating the malignant bug would be to live in a cool climate and work out of doors.

To resign from the bank would be a very big step to take. It would mean leaving a safe job with the prospect of a good pension, eventually. But what if 'eventually' never came? And our financial position was now a little safer. Betsy Tudor, Paulet Tudor's American widow, had recently died and left Harry some money. Not a lot, but enough to make all the difference if we decided to change horses.

Two unexpected events had now happened: the doctor's advice and the legacy. We felt there would surely and inevitably be a third one. And there was. Much to our surprise we were told we could now have a year's leave. Usually leave was due every five years, but practically all the existing Hong Kong Bank staff had started their new terms of duty with the bank in late 1945 or 1946. Obviously they could not all go on leave simultaneously in 1951 so some were given early leave. That included us. Now, most fortuitously, we would have time to consider the future in a leisurely and sensible way.

Two
Hong Kong to Newfoundland via New York

Harry had not seen his father, retired and living permanently in Newfoundland, for sixteen or seventeen years. It seemed an excellent idea to visit him now. The quickest route would be to cross the Pacific and the U.S.A. on our way to St. John's, Newfoundland. Most people returned home on leave by sea in those long-ago days, but luckily the bank had agreed to pay our air fares home to England via the Pacific route. Harry had of course made the long journey out to Hong Kong by flying boat a few years earlier, but this time we were to travel on a series of conventional aircraft.

Our personal household possessions were packed in crates and, together with almost all our clothes, were returned to England by ship. We were informed we could each take only one medium-size, light suitcase and a small flight bag with us on the plane. So two smart, but very light suitcases were especially made. Harry's was conventional tan, mine grey with tan trimmings. It was now October 1948 and, knowing we were to spend three weeks in frozen Newfoundland, we stuffed these two larger cases with warm winter clothing. A knowledgeable friend advised us that as we would be sleeping in the plane for many nights, it would be wise to travel in old, loose, comfortable clothes. So we did.

Casually dressed, we waved goodbye to Hong Kong and took off from Kai Tak in a plane belonging to Philippine Air Lines. It was all very different for both of us from our previous experience of air travel. Harry of course had flown in many different types of aircraft during the War, but never for a long period, except in that flying boat. I had only travelled officially by air twice during the war, from Naples to Algiers and again on the return journey in a Dakota. On the other hand, most unofficially, I had been up in a B-25 Mitchell bomber and a Flying Fortress.

The first plane was to take us as far as Manila. There we would change planes and then proceed to cross the Pacific, which on my atlas looked immense. Our route would be Hong Kong - Manila - Guam - Wake Island - Hawaii - San Francisco, a distance of over nine thousand miles, and in 1948, in a slow plane, it took six or seven days. Harry was delighted to find that the plane to Manila was staffed with some very pretty Filipino air hostesses. He was flirting happily with one of these when, nearing Manila, we hit some turbulence. I started to feel very queasy and shut my eyes as the plane bounced up and down like a yo-yo, but Harry was quite unaffected.

Suddenly I heard the sharp sound of a slap and, opening my eyes, noticed Harry ruefully rubbing a very red cheek. The air hostess had disappeared.

"What happened?" I asked him.

"She hit me," said Harry.

"Why? What did you do?"

"I simply spoke to her in Spanish."

"What did you say?"

"The only sentence I could remember."

"What was that?"

"I just said, '¿Dónde está la cama?'"

"Well, no wonder she slapped you!" I told him. Even I, having like Harry learnt a little Spanish during my last year at school, knew that sentence meant, "Where is the bed?"

Soon after this we landed at Manila airport, the airfield still bearing scars from bombing during the war between Japan and the U.S.A. from 1941 to 1945. The airport buildings, too, were in a ramshackle state, although all the Filipino staff were bedecked in brand-new American military uniforms. The Americans had once again left the Philippine Republic to its own devices.

It was evening and the light was fading. Our next aircraft, which was to fly us in stages across the Pacific, would take off four hours later. So what should we do in the interim?

A Filipino official suggested we took a taxi and went on a sight-seeing tour of Manila. This we did. Although we expected the city to be still war-battered, it was worse than we had anticipated. Very little work had been done in the form of reconstruction. In the diminishing light we saw streets of ruined houses but few people. Nearer the centre of the city there were a few signs of human life and some brightly neon-lit buildings with flashing, coloured lights. At each of the sites our taxi-driver stopped and announced with pride the name of this garish night club. In fact, as far as we were concerned, Manila was just piles of rubble surrounding a cacophony of night clubs … except for one notable exception. Right in the centre of this area of night life the driver stopped again, this time by a large stone monument. In the semi-darkness we recognised the aquiline features of our noble Queen Victoria sitting on a stone throne. Whatever connection did she have with Manila? What on earth was she doing in this squalid city? Victoria was the highlight of our tour of Manila. After we had gazed at her with silent respect, the tax-driver drove us back to the airport.

Luckily there was a different crew on the plane that was to carry us on this long flight across the Pacific, so Harry did not have to confront the outraged air hostess again. We were the only British on board. All the other passengers were Americans returning to their home country, and it was obvious that Philippine Air Lines, P.A.L. for short, were modelling their style on the American way of life.

The seats were comfortable and not squashed too closely together. In fact at night, when the air hostesses came round with a blanket and pillow for each passenger, we found we could recline our seats backward and raise our feet from the floor, or should it be 'deck'? Food was also all-American-style and far too plentiful. Trays of it seemed to appear regularly every two hours. I never knew what meal I was eating and only managed to cope with every other tray. But Harry would not let me refuse a single offering, saying he was quite capable of eating for two. This was true. His unusual capacity for food had always been so. When God created Harry, He left out two important components. One was the ability to feel satiated when he had eaten enough and the other was the ability to actually feel hunger. This meant that he would never feel the pangs of starvation. Likewise, once started, he would never know when to stop eating.

The first refuelling point for the plane itself was the island of Guam, a well-known name from the recent war in the Pacific. Here American uniforms were on show again but with genuine Americans inside them. We all left the plane and more over-abundant food and drink was served to us in the airport building.

Somewhere between Guam and our next stop, Wake Island, Harry celebrated his birthday on October 10th 1948. That day even more food and, naturally, drink, were consumed. Everybody on the plane celebrated Harry's birthday with him. The following day we were told the date was once more October 10th, Harry's birthday again! Why, I asked, did we have two consecutive October 10ths? Because, it was explained, on October 10th we had crossed the International Date Line from west to east, and so had gained a day. If we had crossed the Line from east to west, Harry might not have had a birthday at all that year.

There would be only one more refuelling stop, at Wake Island, before we reached Honolulu. From above, the island appeared to be in the centre of a mini-typhoon. The ubiquitous palm trees had assumed the shape of croquet hoops, their leafy heads bowed to the ground. In fact it seemed safer up above the storm.

But we landed and all the passengers scuttled through the wind and torrential rain into the small airport lounge. Owing to the storm it was dark inside and appeared to be already full of morose figures clutching bottles or glasses. A down-at-heel type came to sit with us and, without preamble or pause for breath, launched, non-stop, into his life story, plus how much he loathed Wake Island and how homesick he was for his wife and family in San Francisco. We bought him several drinks and he made us promise to go to a certain restaurant, apparently his favourite joint, when we reached San Francisco. If we mentioned his name to the owner, we were told, we would receive red-carpet, V.I.P. treatment.

After escaping from this Slough of Despond, our next stop was Honolulu, Hawaii, and Harry's forty-eight hours of birthday celebrations were over. By this time we were both looking exceedingly scruffy, especially me. For several nights we had slept in our clothes and there had been no facilities to wash more than face and hands. Luckily a very friendly American suggested we share a taxi with him and explore some of the island of Oahu instead of promenading in our creased and crumpled state. This was an excellent idea and our taxi-driver took us high up into the hills, stopping every now and then to pick up a guava from the roadside and chuck it into my lap. By the end of the tour I had a whole lapful of fruit which were quite impregnable, green while they should have been pink, and bullet-hard. I left the lot in the taxi.

So we resumed our flight, now on the last leg to San Francisco. It was when we were nearly half-way there that Harry whispered in my ear, "One of the engines has failed. We have turned round and are heading back to Honolulu. Don't say a word to anyone!" As there were only two engines in the comparatively small 1948 aircraft, this seemed a very sensible move. We had not yet reached the 'point of no return'.

Back unexpectedly in Honolulu, Harry and I were given a simple room in a temporary building, which was either a very large Nissen hut or a small aircraft hangar. The room was on the ground floor, and sitting on a bench under the open window were a romantic couple who breathed so heavily and spoke to each other so loudly and ardently that we could not get to sleep. Harry stuck his head out of the window and said, most politely under the circumstances, "Would you kindly move and carry on your conversation somewhere else?" They did. The next morning after a breakfast of fried oysters, a disastrous experiment, we were told we would have to stay in Honolulu for another day and night while they serviced our plane.

We were still wearing our original, recommended, loose, comfortable, elderly clothes and our two large cases were locked in the aircraft. All we had were the small flight bags. Harry, luckily, had packed two clean shirts into his. My bag contained no change of clothes. Generously he offered me one of his clean though creased shirts. I rolled up its sleeves and thrust yards of shirt-tails into my skirt band. Thus attired, clean though crumpled, we set off to see Honolulu.

The airport and harbour still showed signs of the Japanese attack in 1941, but Honolulu itself did not seem to have been much affected. All I had known hitherto about this island was that all the film stars hung out at Waikiki Beach and that everyone who arrived in Hawaii by sea or air was met by beautiful Hula-Hula girls, who festooned visitors with garlands of flowers called Leis and danced for them. But no one had treated us thus.

Harry asked me if I had ever had a Knickerbocker Glory. No, I had not. Well, he told me, I had not lived until I had eaten one. So the first thing we did was to consume two Knickerbocker Glories, very tall glasses containing a rainbow of different-coloured ice creams and fruits. After this the obvious thing to do was to visit Waikiki Beach. We had no bathing costumes, but at the shop we visited I was lucky and found a garish one-piece covered with pictures of Hula-Hula girls, tropical flowers and palm trees. Harry was not so fortunate: the average American male was larger round the middle than he was, so the pair of bathing trunks he was finally forced to buy was very loose round the waist and threatened to slide off his hips. We also bought two beach towels. Now, where could we change? We asked the girl who had served us. She looked at us doubtfully: we were aware we were not looking smart. "You could try the Moana hotel near the beach," she said, "They might let you change there." We sailed confidently into the luxurious premises of the Moana and asked the same question. The snooty man we spoke to said *no*, we definitely could *not* change at the Moana, *period* (full stop). Where then, we asked, could we change? There were *public* changing cubicles for the *hoi polloi*, near the beach, he informed us.

Once garbed in our new swimwear we went to lie on the sand and watched all the lovely girls continuously anointing themselves with sun-cream. These were the girls whose 'bathing costumes never got wet', in the words of a then-popular song. And there were the surf-boarders to observe too. They sailed on the crests of the waves lying or standing on their boards, sometimes on only one leg. It looked quite easy. So why not hire a board and try it ourselves? In my usual cowardly way I insisted on joining Harry on his board. I knew I could not cope on a board alone. We did quite well at first, until I fell off onto some coral, which was very painful. Harry's bathing trunks fortunately did not fall off.

The following day, full of hope, we set off once more for San Francisco. We landed there, crossed the Golden Gate Bridge and arrived in the city at last. American Express had arranged a hotel for us and, reunited with our large suitcases, we were able to change into clean clothes. The restaurant recommended by our morose friend on Wake Island did give us the V.I.P. treatment at lunch, and we set off that evening for the flight across North America.

At the airport we assembled with a large bunch of Americans. All the women were wearing Christian Dior's 'New Look'. Skirts, which had grown steadily shorter during the six years of war, had suddenly plummeted to ankle-length. So every single female except me was wearing a long skirt, a jacket with a nipped-in waist and, unexpectedly, a hat adorned with ostrich feathers. When we were told to board our plane, instead of walking to it in an orderly file, all the ladies picked up their skirts, lowered their heads, held on to their plumed hats and charged towards the aircraft. If they had been holding spears instead of handbags they could have passed for Zulu warriors. Their mates followed. We, feeling very British, sauntered onto the plane and found the only two seats left unoccupied were the worst ones, right up at the front. The American ladies had made their unexpected charge because they wanted to sit in the reputedly safer back seats. We had a miserable, sleepless night. As we were at the front of the cabin, each time someone went to the loo the cabin door opened and a bright light shone in our eyes. I was just beginning to feel sleepy when the plane landed to refuel at Lincoln, Nebraska.

"Come on, we've got to get out now," Harry told me.

"I don't want to get out," I replied.

"Don't you want to see Lincoln, Nebraska?"

"No!"

"Well you've *got* to," he said, hauling me out.

After a sleepless night we reached La Guardia airport the next morning. American Express were supposed to have booked us a hotel room for four nights in New York. Harry rang them and found they had slipped up. This was not surprising as we were two days late. When asked if they could find us another hotel, Harry was told that this particular day was Columbus Day in the U.S.A. and every hotel room in the city was already booked. In despair, Harry then rang the number of a Hong

Kong Bank friend, working in New York. He too seemed very doubtful about our chances, until after racking his brains he said to Harry,

"There is *one* place I know of where you *might* find a room, but it is very, very basic. Know what I mean?"

Harry said he did not care how basic it was; all we wanted was a bed. This mysterious place was apparently called The Lido. We set off in a taxi to our destination. From the outside it looked distinctly unimpressive: a dirty, grey building with many windows but just a small entrance. Inside there was a desk and a man in his shirtsleeves. Harry asked him if he had a vacant double room.

"Yes," said the man, "How many hours?"

"Hours?! I want it for four days!" exclaimed Harry.

The man looked astonished.

"OK," he said, "Here's your key. Want the usual bottle of Bourbon?

"Oh, all right," Harry said, taking the bottle.

Our room was most unprepossessing. There was a ramshackle bed, a shower with a dripping tap, little furniture and it was not clean. Outside in the street a fleet of fire-engines with klaxons wailing at full blast screamed incessantly up and down. But we were so tired we would have slept on a shelf. The bed pinged every time either of us moved a muscle. The tap dripped noisily and every twenty minutes or so, a coloured lady with a bucket and mop opened the door with her key and asked the equivalent of "Can I do you now?" We told her to get lost.

By the following day we had caught up with our sleep. The nature of our 'hotel' was now quite obvious. We discussed it and decided we need only reside there between the hours of midnight and eight a.m. All meals could be eaten elsewhere. In any case the only refreshment the proprietor was prepared to provide was Bourbon.

We purchased sets of wax ear-plugs, which would cut out the sound of fire engines, pinging bed-springs, dripping taps and any other undesirable 'noises off'. Harry took me to an 'Automat' for breakfast: rather like a Lyon's Corner House, but with all the available food visible and locked into separate compartments. No 'Nippies' were employed, so to obtain a chosen item you inserted the correct money in a slot, pulled the handle and out it came. Harry had to remind me to put a beaker under the spout after pressing the knob marked 'Coffee'. I had already poured one lot over the floor.

Being two days late arriving in the U.S.A., it was vital to ring up Russ Wiggins immediately. He was much relieved to hear Harry's voice. The party he and seven other Americans were giving for us was, he said, tomorrow at the Waldorf Astoria hotel at midday. I had a problem. Surprisingly now in the middle of October, New York was experiencing a heat wave. Our suitcases contained clothes, but only for a cold three weeks in Newfoundland. Harry could take off his jacket, but I was most unsuitably dressed in a warm tweed suit and polo-neck sweater. I begged to be allowed to buy just one cool, thin dress with a fashionable New Look long skirt. We went to a well-known New York store and I emerged looking calm and up-to-date, even smart, carrying a carrier bag full of my winter clothes.

That afternoon and evening we visited one of Harry's former girl friends, Betty Carver, now married to a well-known interior decorator. Harry had known her way back in 1931 when he had spent one year working in the New York branch of the Hong Kong Bank. At midnight we slunk back to our sleazy lodgings.

The Americans who were throwing this party for us were all friends Harry had made while serving with M.A.C.A.F. (Mediterranean Allied Coastal Air Force) in Algiers and later at Caserta near Naples. M.A.C.A.F. was made up of R.A.F., U.S.A.A.F. and a few Free French Squadrons. Each R.A.F. officer had to have an American counterpart of exactly equivalent rank. Sometimes they loathed each other, sometimes they got on well. Of the eight men comprising the welcome party I knew only two. One was Colonel Rogers who I had met at a memorable evening at Taranto. I never knew his first name: he was always addressed as "Koynel". The other man was Russ Wiggins.

At Caserta the R.A.F. and nine W.A.A.F. officers shared a Mess with the American officers of M.A.C.A.F. and I got to know Russ well. He was a lovely and remarkable man, and a few words must be said about him. When Harry and I first knew Russ he would have been in his forties. After the War he was Foreign Correspondent for the *Washington Post* and later American Ambassador to the United Nations. He and Harry kept in touch by letter and every Christmas sent each other Christmas greetings in rhyme.

We revolved into the Waldorf Astoria as Noel Coward revolved out, and were taken upstairs to a grand room full of Harry's old friends. I was so relieved to be now wearing a light, summery dress. The magnificent corsage of orchids presented to me would not have looked right pinned on to a Shetland wool sweater. Everyone wanted to know where we were staying but Harry briefed me beforehand:

"If anybody asks you where you're staying, don't for Heaven's sake mention the Lido. Simply say, 'Oh, just a little place off Fifth Avenue.'"

The party was unforgettable with lots to eat and drink, and non-stop reminiscing. It lasted for hours and eventually everybody wanted to drive us 'home'. Somehow we managed to elude this.

The whole of the third day was spent with another of Harry's former girlfriends 'Mary-Lou', now married to Merritt McBrian and living with her three children on Long Island. Merritt was also a former buddy of Harry's and they had invited other friends who remembered him to their house that day.

And then there was just one day left of our brief visit to New York. This was to be nostalgia day for Harry. For me, compared to London, the only other large city I knew well, New York seemed noisier, busier and more friendly. The skyscrapers were imposing, Grand Central Station much cleaner than the grime-encrusted London termini and the streets full of mysterious gratings in the pavements from which emerged clouds of steam. I still remember the actress, Hermione Gingold's, explanation of these emissions of steam. In her deep, gravelly voice she said they were caused by "All the Red Indians down below, smoking their pipes".

So on this last day Harry took me to visit, mainly on foot, many of the places he had known in 1931. These included the Hong Kong Bank in Wall Street, Central Park, the garage where he had bought his first American second-hand car and last of all the Empire State Building. We whizzed up at great speed in a lift and at the top gazed at New York to the north, south, east and west. Then we found a booth where you could make a gramophone record. This we did, quite unrehearsed, speaking rubbish in turn in breathless voices. We sounded as if we had just climbed all the way to the top by stairs. That record is still around, somewhere.

Three
Newfoundland

Now the time had come to leave New York for what was our reason for making this long journey by air from Hong Kong: for Harry to see his father. Hugh had visited his family in England occasionally in the 1930's but had not seen Harry, who was then working in the Far East.

Once more we took to the air and flew to Gander, where we changed into a smaller plane which took us to St. John's, the capital of the then Dominion of the British Empire. Newfoundland became a province of Canada the following year, 1949.

At the airport to meet us was one of Harry's former R.A.F. Intelligence Officers, junior in rank though not in age. This was Josh O'Driscoll, and he greeted us with the remark, "My God, don't you two look alike!" We eyed each other with horror. He took us to our hotel, thankfully a complete contrast to the Lido: modern, clean and utterly respectable.

And then we went to see Harry's father, the retired Major General Sir Henry Hugh Tudor K.C.B., C.M.G. I had never met him, only seen many photographs of him, always in uniform or astride a horse. I wondered if this senior Army officer would be unapproachable. But I was greeted kindly. Luckily, while serving in the Army in India between the Boer and Great Wars, he had met three of my father's brothers. Uncles Ernest, Clement and Gerald were all Army Officers who loved horses, polo and riding in races against each other. So in Hugh's eyes they were 'good chaps' and I took on some of their respectability. It was surprising that he was such a little man. In his photographs he looked of average height but now, obviously due to osteoporosis, he had shrunk by four or five inches. He was crippled too with arthritis and only able to move slowly and painfully on crutches. But he was

43

Major General Sir Henry Hugh Tudor

impeccably dressed with a small military moustache and quite a substantial head of white hair. Being so physically handicapped he had a permanent and devoted nurse living with him: Monnie McCarthy. As well as caring for her patient, Monnie was also housekeeper and cook. They were living in a small flat, just large enough for two, on the hill behind St. John's. Life must at that time have been rather dull for Hugh, as he could no longer go out. But he kept in touch with the outside world with the aid of an enormous radio set, which seemed capable of receiving every possible world radio station. Fortunately one of his great talents was languages and he could understand most of the transmissions. This was now his great hobby.

One of the reasons for our visit was that he had recently had cataracts removed from both eyes. In those days that was a major operation. He had spent three weeks in St. John's Hospital after this operation, lying on a bed between sandbags and unable to move a muscle. But it had been worth it. Formerly almost totally blind, he was now able to see his son again.

Apart from Harry's friend Josh O'Driscoll there was one person I thought I might see again in St. John's. This went back to my schooldays at what must have been the prototype for 'St. Trinians'. One of the pupils there had been a girl called Margaret Baird and for some terms I had shared a bedroom with her and three others. After 'lights out' when talking was prohibited, she would tell us in a loud whisper all about her father's departmental store, the great 'Baird's Store' in St. John's, Newfoundland. To me it sounded most impressive, a cross between Harrods and Selfridges, with probably a Union Jack flying from the roof. Undoubtedly her father must have been very well off as he had sent both his son and his daughter to be educated in England and they only went home for the long summer holidays. Also Margaret's pocket money, five times as much as most of us had, was always in the form of gold sovereigns, which I had never seen before.

45

By coincidence there was a Canadian girl from Montreal, Peggy Cape, also at this small school. We wore little uniform except for gym and games, and on Sundays processed to church twice, wearing any kind of coat, although a small, round hat was compulsory. Margaret and Peggy appeared dressed in their fur coats for church on cold Sundays, and impressed us all.

Harry and I inspected downtown St. John's where the harbour and all the shops were. I had imagined St. John's might be rather like Folkestone, with a harbour and possibly a promenade, large stone houses and reasonable shops. And the largest and most impressive would, of course, be Baird's Department Store. It was a great surprise to see that all the old buildings, including most of the shops, were built of wood. So Baird's Store was a wooden building, full of different departments, true, but each one very small. Not at all what I had expected. I asked in the store if Margaret Baird was still living on the island and was told that she was, though no longer Margaret Baird as she had married a doctor.

So Margaret and I met again. She and her paediatrician husband lived in a luxurious flat half-way up the hill behind old St. John's. They had two very small children. It must have been a great surprise for her that one of her junior schoolmates had tracked her down. When I told her I was married to Harry Tudor she behaved as if I had said I had married the Prince of Wales. In the very small population of Newfoundland, about 570,000 in all, the Governor and Harry's father were equal in eminence. We were invited to dinner with Margaret and her husband and then entertained them at the hotel, but that was that. Many years had elapsed since our schooldays and we did not have much else in common.

It was the hospitable O'Driscoll family, Josh, his wife Amy and their four children, who took us to their hearts and into their private family circle. Every day we visited Hugh and his nurse, Monnie, in their warm little flat, but there was a limit to the conversation-time before Hugh grew tired. The O'Driscolls' became our second home. They welcomed us into their typical Canadian-style house with the garage and boiler room at ground level and all the other rooms above. It had to be a large house as the three sons and one daughter still lived at home. Josh and Amy showed us round part of the island, sadly short of roads, in which there seemed to be but two industries, fishing and timber. And we were entertained at their cabin in the woods where they always spent part of the summer. One of the sons ran the local dance band, which played for dances and at the single night club. Many evenings we followed the band.

The snow season had started and we were glad now of our warm winter clothes. In Baird's Store (where else?) we discovered warm leather ankle-boots with fur linings. Harry bought a pair for me and also for himself. We would never find anything like this in England, so he splashed out on a pair for his mother and a pair for each of his three sisters.

Most of our meals were at the hotel and could not be faulted except for the unusually slow service between the courses. But we had no reason to hurry, so Harry suggested we put the waiting time to good use. He was a bit shocked that I knew not one word of my mother's native language, and suggested that we should teach ourselves Danish. Like his father, Harry was a natural linguist and enjoyed learning new languages. I found it tedious. The versatile Baird's Store provided two Teach-Yourself Danish/Norwegian books. Apparently both countries spoke the same language so we would be learning two for the price of one. Our fellow hotel guests must have been baffled by our behaviour. In between courses we declaimed, in Danish, useful sentences such as,

"Good morning! I trust you have had a restful sleep?"

"Excuse me, sir! Would you be so kind as to direct me to the Opera?"

Harry at least did a very credible imitation of a Danish accent.

As our three weeks' stay in St. John's drew to an end we heard ominous remarks about it now being the 'iceberg season'. Oh, how I wished we were continuing this last, short leg of our journey to England by air, but for some very good reason, now forgotten, we were crossing the North Atlantic by sea.

It was distressing for Harry and Hugh to have to say goodbye to each other. Each knew they would probably never meet again. I too felt sad at leaving the dear, frail old man, so far away from his family. Of his four children only Elizabeth and Harry had crossed the ocean to visit him, and that infrequently. But though now an old seventy-seven, he actually lived to ninety-four.

Four
Return to England

Our little boat, pocket-sized compared to the liners previously travelled in, was one of the Furness-Withy line plying to and fro between Liverpool and St. John's. The S.S. Duddon was barrel-shaped and, like a barrel, it rolled.

As soon as we left the shelter of St. John's harbour the Duddon started to lurch from side to side. It was difficult not to think of the Titanic and mountainous icebergs. At dinner on the first night the fiddles were already in position round the dining tables: a sinister sign, and this was the last sighting we had of the majority of our fellow passengers for several days. At night the ship rocked from side to side and we had to brace ourselves against the sides of the two bunks to avoid falling on to the floor. Simultaneously, with each roll, our suitcases slid across the floor between the bunks crashing into the woodwork. But we were not seasick. We reckoned we must be good sailors.

For several days most passengers were confined to their cabins. But Harry and I ventured outside and discovered a convenient square deck at one end of the ship; it must have been the blunt end. Luckily it was quite empty; in fact there was no sign of a human being anywhere. For the sake of our health we marched up and down and round and round this space, singing at the top of our voices. The song we sang most, with arms entwined round each other's waists, was *Hi! Diddle-Dee-Dee - An Actor's Life For Me!* which comes from Walt Disney's *Pinnochio*, and was originally sung by a thespian fox. It was a very good tune to march to. As we drew nearer to British waters the rest of our fellow passengers emerged at last from their cabins, paler and thinner.

Liverpool was our port. Elizabeth, Harry's eldest sister, was living then in the Wirral, so firstly we went to stay with her.

We had much enjoyed our protracted journey from Hong Kong to England, but at the back of our minds, all the time, had been the unresolved problem: should we return to the Hong Kong Bank when the year's leave was over? Or should we throw in our hand for the sake of Harry's health and take up an outdoor life in England? That had been the Hong Kong Bank doctor's advice to rid Harry of the malaria bug.

By this time we had both decided on the latter plan. Harry was very attracted by the idea of farming, but this seemed rather unrealistic. We were aware we knew little or nothing about farming; however my brother Guy had recently finished a one-year ex-serviceman's agricultural course. If he agreed to join us it could be just possible. Also thanks to Betsy Tudor's bequest to Harry in her Will we would have, hopefully, enough money to buy a very modest farm.

We arranged to meet Guy and put this proposal to him. The idea suited him well, and we agreed to spend three years as a threesome, dividing any profits made three ways. All of us would contribute equal efforts at being farm labourers. Guy would also contribute the knowledge gained on his course and his experience with pigs pre-war. He also knew how to milk a cow. Harry would contribute the cost of buying the farm and stocking it. He also knew quite a lot about horses. I would contribute my knowledge of cooking and bottle-washing. I also knew quite a lot about poultry, thanks to my father. Since Guy had done the course, he would be the boss and we would do what we were told.

Five
Fools Rush In

"Is everything satisfactory, Mrs. Tudor?" enquired Mrs. Morris, proprietress of the "Waverley Private Hotel" in Hereford. She had that 'don't you dare complain' look on her face.

"Yes, thank you, Mrs. Morris ... but there is just one small thing ... it's awfully cold in our bedroom."

Mrs. Morris looked astonished.

"Cold? I don't understand that at all. After all, your room is over Miss Foster's."

I thought about Miss Foster, an elderly, bony lady, who always wore at least four jumpers and cardigans.

"She doesn't give off much heat," I replied.

Harry, Guy and I were all staying at this boarding house. It was by now November 1948. All three of us liked the idea of a Herefordshire farm; hence our stay at the Waverley Hotel while we searched. But though cheap, it was a dismal dump.

The only warm place was the steamy basement kitchen, where we and all the other inmates had our meals sitting round a scrubbed kitchen table. Poor Mrs. M. was finding it hard to cope with the minute food and coal rations. Breakfast was the best meal: first porridge, which was nice and filling, then occasionally a kipper or a boiled egg. The eggs also tasted strongly of kipper because the discarded skins were fed to Mrs. M.'s hens, who lived in the back garden. She counted the slices of bread we ate and the cups of tea she poured.

"A *third* cup of tea, Mr. Tudor?" she would ask.

The residents' lounge had a small fireplace, and in it a tiny fire was allowed to burn. No resident was permitted to touch the fire, move the fire irons, or even brush up any ashes. Mrs. M. would enter silently every half hour or so and observe her lodgers crouched round the little flickering flame. Soundlessly she would place two small pieces of coal on the fire, brush up a spoonful of ashes, re-arrange the fire-irons correctly - just so - and without saying a word, glide out again.

A furnished cottage to rent became available in a village near Ross-on-Wye and we seized the chance to become independent. There was a good supply of logs to burn in its open fireplace and we were warmer. But the minuscule food rations were an even greater problem here, for now I was responsible for feeding two hungry men.

At that time rationing was at its most stringent. Every item of a basic diet was rationed: meat, bacon, butter, sugar, cheese, eggs, milk, tea and even potatoes and bread. It was worse than wartime.

"Never mind," said Guy, "When we've started farming Harry and I will get extra cheese."

"What about me?" I asked.

"Oh, they don't give extra cheese to women. Not unless they're land girls."

"Well, I don't think that's fair. I bet the farmer's wife works just as hard as the men!" I felt affronted.

"I shouldn't worry. After six months or so we'll be self-sufficient. Own milk, eggs, potatoes, chickens, rabbits, bacon, ham, bread, butter, cheese, etc." Guy said confidently.

"Who's going to make all this 'bread, butter and cheese'?"

"You are of course."

In Ross-on-Wye we discovered a partial solution to the feeding problem. Down a side street was an eating place called *Alf's Café*. Its windows were always obscured by steam and a dingy piece of net curtain, but outside on one of them Alf had written in chalk, 'Alf's Café - Always a Meal.' So we filled ourselves up at Alf's several times a week.

We were lucky to find a suitable farm so quickly, and the 'land flowing with milk and honey' became a possibility. It was a hundred-acre mixed farm, which meant it was partly arable and partly grass. It was then we bought our first instruction book, of which many more were to follow, called *Farming, How to Start*. We all studied this. Having no car we also purchased three sturdy, new bicycles. Mine was of the sit-up-and-beg variety and I attached a huge bicycle basket to its handlebars. It had no gears and there were many hills to climb on our journeys from the cottage to the new farm. How I wish that bicycles with gears had been available in 1949.

While waiting to get possession, we would cycle over daily to Broad Oak to tend the few animals that were included in the price of the farm. Just beyond the little village on the left-hand side of the road to Monmouth was a gate with a sign on it saying 'Caldicott Fm' - that was all the signwriter had had room for. From the agent's particulars it had sounded just what we wanted. Right size, right position and most importantly, right price. The descriptive blurb went into raptures about the fields, some of them level and some sloping downhill to the south east. Most were now arable because the War Agricultural Executive Committee, or 'War Ag.' for short, still wielded power and paid two pounds per acre for permanent pasture, ploughed up to grow crops.

The buildings sounded adequate, including the 'late 14th century cowsheds, stables and pig sties, the commodious barns and the cattle-yard with surrounding shelters supported on stone pillars.'

But when it came to the description of the interior of the farmhouse, the agent had been suspiciously brief. He had also deleted every vowel from most of the nouns, so all it said was: '16th C. House, with Ktchn, Sclry, 2 Strms, Lrdr, Dry Cllr, 5 Bds and capacious Atts. No Mains Water or Electricity.'

Since the last owner - a very eccentric bachelor - had died, the land had been farmed by a man from North Herefordshire, but he had not lived

53

in the house. Also included in the sale price were numerous antiquated farm implements, mostly hidden in brambles and high weeds. These were all suitable for using with a horse, and the horse was part of the deal too. She was called 'Poppy' and was almost as ancient as the implements. The locals said she was at least thirty years old.

Accompanying Poppy were her friends the cows, and we were taking them on as well. I had never seen such a motley, bedraggled and gormless looking crew. They could have come straight out of *Cold Comfort Farm* and I mentally christened them 'Feckless', 'Graceless', 'Hopeless' and 'Clueless', although none of them appeared to have a wooden leg. These ladies had been used as nurse cows to rear Hereford-cross calves and were all Shorthorns except for one who looked brighter and more intelligent than the others. She became known as 'Amy the amiable Ayrshire.'

Six
Caldicott Farm

On our first inspection of the farm it was Guy who had taken charge.

"We'll see the land first," he told the agent.

This was a complete reversal of the status quo. Three years earlier we had all been in the R.A.F.: Harry a Wing Commander, I a W.A.A.F. Officer and Guy a Corporal. I was then required to look up to Harry and address him as 'sir'. Guy would have done so too, and been obliged as well to call me, his sister, 'ma'am', if we were both in uniform. Now the boot was on the other foot and I daresay Guy, in his quiet way, was enjoying it.

We walked round the entire farm with the agent who was rather desperately pointing out any good feature he could think of.

"Here's the brook that forms part of your boundary," he told us when we reached the lowest section of the little wood called 'Popland's Brake.' "Never been known to run dry this brook, so your animals will have good clean water in four fields."

He seemed keen on water, and when we came to the paddock in front of the house, showed us a very muddy pool.

"Lovely pond that! Just the place for the farmer's wife's ducks. Eh? Now under here," he said, pointing to an old hand pump against the side of the house, "is a famous well. I can see you're wondering why it's famous? It's because it has never in living memory been known to fail!"

Just as well, I thought. The particulars had stated starkly, 'Water by well', and in small print at the very end, 'The accuracy of these particulars cannot be guaranteed.' It could have been worse. Years later we were to inspect another farm where the details said even more baldly: 'Water by rain.'

Two views of Caldicott Farm

"May we see the house now, Guy?" I asked hopefully, as we were standing near the back door.

"No, not yet. Do be patient Sonia. We're going to look at the buildings next."

The buildings had been most accurately described as 'mediæval.' They really deserved to be in some farm museum.

"These are the fourteenth-century stables," the agent declaimed, indicating a black space minus a ceiling; the loft floor had rotted away. "And this is the cow-shed."

"That's where you would milk your cows, Harry," said Guy.

"*My* cows?" Harry looked surprised. He didn't know one end of a cow from the other.

"Yes. You are going to be in charge of all the cows and cattle generally. I, of course, am going to deal with the pig side and Sonia will look after the poultry section."

This was the first we had heard of division of labour, and poor Harry had drawn the short straw.

Then after inspecting the fourteenth-century pig sties, all the other historic farm buildings, and glancing at the new Dutch barn and tractor shed, we were at last going to see the house, which would be my province.

I could not wait to look inside. We entered by the back door, straight into the 'Sclry'. This was a cavernous, stone-flagged space, completely empty except for a puzzling hole in the middle of the floor.

"What's that hole for?" I asked.

"For throwing slops down," replied the agent.

"Where does it drain to?"

"I've no idea," he said.

The kitchen was a bit better. Two large windows, a rusty, old, black cooking range, the traditional, massive built-in dresser and a puzzling little iron door high up in the thick wall on the right-hand side of the range. This turned out to be an old bread oven.

I will not go into a long description of the rest of the house, but though hardly 'ideal home' material, I thought it had possibilities and what house agents call 'potential'. When we noticed the old plaster Tudor rose in the middle of the sitting room ceiling, it seemed a good omen.

However there were a lot of 'no's': no mains water, no electricity, no telephone, no indoor loo, no bathroom and no sink in the so-called scullery. This meant all water had to be pumped by hand, and lighting was by paraffin lamps and candles. Quite a long way down the garden path, in what the agent optimistically described as the 'kitchen garden', was the outdoor earth closet. It was really rather a fine specimen, fourteenth century perhaps? A three-seater with suitably sized accommodation for mum, dad and one child. But a long way to trek on a cold, stormy night.

So it seemed we would have to revert to living and farming like Harry's Tudor forebears. Luckily we were all full of pioneering spirit at the time and quite prepared to rough it.

Just before we moved in we added three improvements. First the telephone. We became 'St. Weonards 45'. and as it was pre-dialling days, when we picked up the 'phone we found ourselves talking to a formidable-sounding lady, whom we privately called 'Mrs. St. Weonards'. We never met her or discovered her real name.

"St. Weonards!" she would croak, "What number do you want?"

"Could you put me through to St. Weonards 36 please?"

"Won't be anyone answering there today. They've gone to Gloucester. Try this evening."

"Thank you very much." I put the receiver back gently. I did not want to jar her ear.

Then we partitioned off part of the scullery and a plumber installed a W.C. and a wash-basin, which in some way, although I never understood how, were connected to the outside pump. I remember you had to rush out and do ten pumps after each flush. Mains water was definitely going to arrive very soon, we were told, and then we could have a bathroom as well. 'Preece the plumber', who was to become a good friend, also installed a sink with taps and draining boards under the window in the empty space of the scullery, the hole in the floor was filled in and it began to look like a scullery.

The third improvement was to rip out the beautiful but useless old cast-iron range. I would have loved an Aga or an Esse, and been quite pleased with a Rayburn, but these were either much too expensive or unobtainable. So we settled for a modern, green cooking stove called 'The Insulated Crag'. If you remove the 'a' from 'insulated' it becomes 'insulted', which the Crag often was. The cooker had two ovens and its top was covered with little, round, removable flue covers, as it was very prone to soot. The instructions told us to feed it with anthracite. We could not get enough of this expensive rationed fuel, so we stuffed it with coal, wood and rubbish as well. It would devour them all - when in the mood. But if fed with too much rubbish it would become a very insulted Crag indeed. Then it either went out, became red-hot with fury all over its top, or set the chimney on fire. This, though alarming and dangerous, had the advantage of disposing of all the accumulated soot, so no chimney sweep was ever required.

When moving-in day came, the furniture arrived from Norwich where it had been in store since 1941. It belonged jointly to Guy and me and we divided it up as amicably as possible. Guy's half was then put in the attic. I found my half contained three settees and four armchairs, but no dining-room furniture.

It was a most unharmonious collection, but then it always had been. Some was from our mother's flat. She had bought it during her 'modern Italian furniture' period and, although it had come from Heals, it was garishly painted in bright hues and further decorated with multicoloured flowers. In contrast all her sitting-room furniture was funereal black.

Added to this were our father's more conventional pieces and some plain but serviceable 1930's stuff. We were lucky to have it. The only alternative would have been post-war 'utility' furniture which was shoddy and nasty. We solved the dining-room table problem by laying an old door we had found in the granary over some trestles in the big hall and covering it with an army blanket.

The grandfather clock also lived in the hall. We placed it strategically in a corner where its various noises could not be heard by sleepers upstairs. It was not the chimes that bothered us - they were quite melodious - but its unsociable habit of growling and grumbling to itself noisily for a full five minutes before it struck the hour. My father had been so fond of this old long-case clock. He had bought it in Baldock, when he was a young man, and its maker's name and the date, 1795, were engraved inside the back.

The official front door, not often used, led out of the hall into the front garden. It was still the original sixteenth-century door, immensely thick and had neither key nor bolt. Instead it was secured by a long, solid length of wood, which was inserted into two deep holes on either side of the interior side of the door. It would have needed many strong men and a battering ram to break it down.

I remember the Caldicott kitchen with nostalgia. We had to furnish it in a haphazard way with whatever we already had. So the two high-backed, cushioned basket chairs, considered suitable for servants pre-war, sat on either side of the Crag cooker. The cats loved them and fought each other for sitting and lying space. They were often forced to arrange themselves in several layers. Two small sprung benches obliged as window seats, fitting perfectly into the alcoves beneath each window. The dresser housed all our china on its shelves and hooks, and there were two large, scrubbed kitchen tables to eat at or work on. A tall clothes horse along the wall on the left of the cooker and assorted kitchen chairs completed the equipment. The telephone rested on a windowsill, since the kitchen was undoubtedly the heart of this home. It was a real kitchen, for living in, not a modern, clinical, germ-free laboratory.

To start with Guy was the 'gaffer'. He had been on this twelve-month farming course, after all. Even before that he had known quite a lot about pigs and also how to hand-milk a cow. Harry and I knew practically nothing, although I had learnt two invaluable skills from my father: one was how to skin a rabbit. This was very useful as they were to be our main item of diet. The other was how to dislocate a chicken's neck when necessary, without having to resort to strangulation. But looking back we do not think Guy had quite got the hang of some of the instructions on his farming course. Harry always did what he was told, but wondered why, on occasions, it was necessary for him to gallop along beside the tractor being driven by Guy?

They were both beginning to look a bit agricultural by now: Guy in his rather fine but worn leather jerkin, ripped in places, Harry in an old ex-G.I. jacket with torn pockets and a peaked cap, which had rapidly become so impregnated with cow's hair and general muck that it had assumed the shape of his head, like a plaster cast. Even when not being worn it retained its rounded appearance and looked like Harry.

What should the well-dressed farmer's wife wear? I consulted the back pages of *The Farmers Weekly* and *Farmer and Stockbreeder* for the answer to this question. These few pages were devoted, rather patronisingly I thought, to the farmer's wife and her interests. From them it appeared she was entirely preoccupied with poultry and making nourishing stews and pies for her menfolk. As for clothes the advertisements always showed her wearing a variety of hip-length smocks: spotted, striped

Sonia at the door with Guy

Sonia with co-workers

or flowered. As they only revealed her top half, I never discovered what she wore below, if anything. I decided smocks were not for me and studied my fellow farmers' wives. They seemed to wear layers of pinnies and aprons. Mrs. Williams from Cwm Madoc, next door, was very large and wore a long black tent that swept the floor. But then, owing to her girth it was unlikely that she did more than throw scraps to her hens outside in the yard. I decided to copy the land girls and wear bib-and-brace dungarees.

I knew I had been appointed Head of the Poultry Section, but that was not all. My other jobs were the housework, cooking, shopping by bicycle, decorating, cleaning and filling the many paraffin lamps and heaters, gardening and egg-washing. Also, helping with harvesting, hay-making and cutting savoy cabbages in winter and, almost the last straw, lending a hand with the threshing when the threshing machine arrived.

So why did I not get extra cheese? It still rankles!

Seven
The Land, the Milk and the Honey

Meanwhile we had started to stock the farm. A few better-grade animals were added to the gang of disreputable old nurse cows, and little Hereford bull calves were bought at Hereford Market for them to suckle. Harry learned how to milk and, after the calves had had their fill, he took what milk we wanted for the house. Any remaining was fed to the little pigs.

Having a rather facetious imagination, I thought of the animals Harry was responsible for as the 'Cattle Command'.

It followed therefore, that Guy was in charge of the 'Pig Platoon'. For this he bought a magnificent Large White boar with a most impressive pedigree, whose official name was 'Howie Dainty Boy 15th', a name more suitable for a Chihuahua than a great, hulking boar pig. We provided him with four young wives for starters.

Now it was my turn, and the 'Poultry Patrol' was presented with a brown Leghorn/Rhode Island Red cross-bred cockerel and twenty-five matching point-of-lay pullets. That cockerel came to a very sticky end. I will tell his story later.

But that was not all. The Poultry Patrol was also introduced to a thing called, at different times, either a 'chick brooder', a 'hover' or a 'foster mother'. I can best describe it as a kind of large imitation hen. In the centre was a capricious paraffin heater round which there was space for a hundred chicks. It had a metal lid with a hole in the middle, and the whole apparatus was enclosed by strips of green felt, simulating hens' feathers. The chicks could walk through these out into an enclosed area containing their food and drink, and then back underneath nice, green, warm 'Mum'.

"Now Sonia, this is quite simple," said Guy, speaking slowly, and as far as possible in words of one syllable.

"All you have to do is:
1) Fill the container with paraffin;
2) Light the wick;
3) Then adjust it to the right height to give the chicks the correct temperature."

"What is the correct temperature?"

"The same as they'd have beneath a hen, stupid! Then you put the chicks underneath. That's all there is to it. Do you understand?"

"Yes, I think so, Guy."

I decided I would have to find some kind of thermometer, stick it under a broody hen, see what temperature she was running at and adjust the wick to match.

The first hundred day-old chicks, all pullets, soon arrived from Sterling Poultry Products, and I set off on the long chick-rearing trail that was to last for years. We had an outing to Sterling's, first to see the eggs in incubators and then to witness the hatching. But what fascinated me most was the Japanese chick sexer. It was not his looks I found fascinating, but his job. At that time only the Japanese knew how to sex chicks. How they did it was a jealously guarded mystery and so far no-one from Japan had divulged the secret. So each hatchery had to have one resident Japanese gentleman to perform this unusual task. Someone must have spilt the beans eventually, because a few years later we found an ordinary Englishman doing the job, and not a Japanese person in sight. This particular Oriental was working at the rate of one chick per second. All the little pullet chicks were sorted into trays on his right and the cockerel chicks into trays on his left. Poor little cockerels: most of them had pitifully short lives. They were fed almost immediately to pigs.

As soon as our first batch of chicks had outgrown their artificial mother and were wearing feathers, the survivors moved out to make way for another lot. I have to say 'survivors', because some always got crushed to death if the hover did not give off enough heat. Others were cremated when it became too hot. I said it was capricious, didn't I?

Before the war, when living at home in Norfolk, we had had three gundogs. They used to get very muddy out shooting and needed frequent baths. For this my father bought a large zinc bath - I think it was called a 'bungalow bath' - and in it I used to wash the dogs. My father would hold them down because they always objected strongly and, wearing a raincoat back to front for protection, I would do the shampooing. The dogs rinsed themselves by jumping into the small river that ran past the bottom of our field.

Now that bath was going to be used again, but by humans this time, as we all got very dirty going about our allotted duties with cattle, pigs and poultry, and the field work as well. Of course we could have emulated the lady in *Lark Rise to Candleford* and washed 'up as far as possible' one day and 'down as far as possible' the next. But it was more pleasant to do it all in one go in a bath.

So the old bungalow bath was brought into the kitchen every night and placed in front of the stove. Then every saucepan and kettle we possessed was set to heat on the Crag. When really hot, all the water was poured into the bath, cold water added as desired, and the lucky bather would climb in and wallow, as far as possible in its rather limited space. We took it in turns, one person every evening, and after his or her ablutions, that person had to bale all the water out and throw it down the drain in the scullery. How I enjoyed those baths! With the soft, yellow glow of an oil lamp on one side and a pink gleam from the stove on the other, it was heavenly. I always emerged feeling far cleaner and better scrubbed than from any conventional bath with hot and cold running water.

We were still anxiously awaiting the arrival of the promised mains water. In the meantime we had to do a lot of pumping. It was summer now, and it became necessary to get extra help to harvest some crops. A bus-load of young men and women was sent for the day, from a local 'Agricultural Holiday Camp.' All their time seemed to be spent rolling around together in the hedgerows, or whiling away the hours visiting our single loo. That was the reason for my non-stop pumping. Remember: 'one flush equals ten pumps,' and there was a never-ending queue outside the back door. Harry came along at mid-morning and saw me in action.

"How about some tea for the workers?"

"Tea?" I snarled, "I daren't stop pumping. You do realise what will happen if we fill them up with tea, don't you?"

"I'll take over the pump," he said. "You go in and make several gallons of tea, there's a good girl."

When the mains water finally arrived, Preece the plumber returned and installed drinking troughs in every field for the animals. For us he made a lovely new bathroom with all modern conveniences. We carved the bathroom out of part of the granary that formed the west side of the house. Now unlimited mains water, hot and cold, gushed out of several taps, and the faithful old zinc bath was hung up in an outdoor shed. Preece and his men worked hard and when they had finished he tried to explain the working of the new septic tank. It was beyond me, but I do remember him saying, "The effluent from a properly constructed septic tank is fit to drink." I would take his word for it.

Eight
Chinkie

Mothers-in-law are an old music hall joke, and the relationship between a wife and her mother-in-law or a husband and his, can be fraught with peril.

This was true for me, although as my own mother was dead, Harry did not have the problem. But what does one call one's mother-in-law? Mine would not have tolerated being addressed as 'Eva' and I certainly was not going to call her Lady Tudor. Then we had a brainwave. As a young girl she had belonged to a sketching and painting club. Each member had had to have a *nom-de-plume* - or perhaps in this case, it was more a *nom-de-brosse* - and hers had been 'Chinkie'. That would do nicely.

Chinkie was a lady of great character and determination, but with a most endearing eccentricity. She still lived in the past, partly in the Victorian days of her privileged childhood and partly, I estimated, in the 1920's. Anyhow, it was a novelty for her to have her only son now actually living in England, as he had been abroad for most of the previous fifteen years. So she came to visit us very soon after we moved into Caldicott. The initial lack of basic 'mod. cons.' did not deter her at all. It was thanks to her that we now had a few nice pieces of antique furniture as well as enough pictures in huge, ornate frames to fill an art gallery. The pictures were surplus to her requirements and surplus to ours too. They were stored for the time being in the open-floored part of the granary.

Chinkie roamed around with her camera taking photographs of work on the farm, many featuring Harry and Poppy the carthorse. She also set up her easel in various places and painted some very good watercolours. When she returned home to Bury St. Edmunds, she

Harry on Poppy

Poppy, Harry and Sonia

had her snaps printed, and then enlarged the best, and hand painted those. Her skies and landscapes were lovely, but animals and people were not her strong point. So we have many pictures of Poppy in action, wearing extra long ears and looking more like a mule, and of cows who could easily be mistaken for very fat reindeer.

In the front of the house was a small walled garden consisting mainly of an unpromising square of rough grass. The unmended gap in the lower stone wall had allowed cows to enter, and the ground was pock-marked by their hooves. Even after the wall had been rebuilt, both cows and pigs seized every chance to enter if either of the two gates was left open for a minute. They would eat or uproot every tender plant. Now I understood why farmers were notoriously non-gardeners. There was little growing there when we arrived, apart from a Japanese quince, an old 'Gloire de Dijon' climbing rose against the house wall, a laburnum, a few shrubs and a small, weedy flower bed. The north wall was almost entirely occupied by a large wood shed. I always thought that this must be where 'Aunt Ada Doom saw something nasty'.

One day I set off to shop in Ross, and Chinkie offered to do some gardening for me while I was away. I left her to it thankfully; she was a very good gardener. On my return I could hear a voice muttering away in the front garden. It was saying, "We don't want this ... we don't need that, and we certainly don't want those."

I opened the door in the garden wall. There stood Chinkie with a heap of rejects and weeds on the path, and just a few lonely-looking plants left standing in the flower bed. As yet more were flung onto the pile of discards, I felt a little sad: I had thought those plants rather pretty.

Later I sorted out that piece of garden myself, in an amateurish way. A new lawn was laboriously hand-sown, square by square, using many bamboo canes to mark my progress. A stone path was laid down the middle, with a long rose bed on either side. Easy annuals like godetias, clarkias and larkspurs were planted and I had beginner's luck with a packet of pink mallows called 'Lavatera Loveliness.' They prospered and flourished exceedingly well, but that first summer at Caldicott Harry would always disgrace me when we had visitors. He used to entice them into the garden saying, "You must come and see Sonia's lovely lavatories." I could have brained him.

By now we had got to know our neighbour on the south side, David Williams from Cwm Madoc farm. He was a dear, kind man who still had all his eleven children from two marriages living at home. Our predecessor at Caldicott had had an arrangement with David to take his 'bulling' cows to the Cwm Madoc bull, and this privilege was transferred to us.

One evening during Chinkie's first visit, Guy told Harry that one of our cows was in this interesting state and that they must take her round to Cwm Madoc immediately. It happened to be suppertime and I had gone out to tell them that food was ready. I found them both in the cattle yard. All the cows were there, including the one who was feeling so passionate. She was in such a state of excitement that she would not let herself be caught to have a halter put on her, and was behaving in a very indecorous way.

"What do we do if we can't catch her?" asked Harry.

"You'll have to lasso her", said Guy.

"Well, I know I spent a year in America," replied Harry, "but one of the things I *didn't* learn was how to lasso a cow!"

Still he went off and returned with a very long rope with a running noose on the end. I was most intrigued by all this and was watching from the safe side of the cattle yard gate. To our great surprise, Harry eventually succeeded in throwing the loop round the amorous cow's neck, but this further excited the animal and she took off round the yard, dragging Harry with her. There were open-sided shelters all round this area, but in the centre was an open midden. Owing to rain it was now full of very wet muck. Poor Harry, who had lost his footing, was being dragged through this by the agitated cow. But he would not let go of the rope.

At this point Chinkie arrived, picking her way daintily between the cowpats. She needed to know what was holding up the serving of supper. Even when staying in pre-historic farmhouses like ours, she still kept up her standards. So she was wearing a long 'tea-gown' of the 1920's era. It was made of velvet and had a narrow band of fur down both sides of the wrap front and round the neck and sleeves. I can just remember my mother wearing these garments: a kind of cross between a dressing-gown and an evening dress. Hers had been rather more frivolous, often made of a diaphanous, peach-coloured crêpe-de-chine. When thus attired she would recline full length on a settee with her feet up, holding a Russian cigarette in one hand and a cocktail in the other. Chinkie joined me at the gate and saw Harry lying on his stomach, being towed around in the mire.

"My dear boy, what *are* you doing?" she enquired. But Harry, wisely, did not open his mouth to explain.

At last the cow calmed down a bit, and Harry and Guy together set out with her to Cwm Madoc. Somehow, as they left the yard, she managed to jerk herself free and, with halter dangling, dashed up the lane, onto the road and turned left for Cwm Madoc. She had been there before and knew perfectly well where the bull lived. She was waiting impatiently outside the bull's pen and bellowing her head off when they arrived.

Meanwhile, back at Caldicott the tin bath was brought out and filled with hot water. Someone was going to need a bath before he had any supper that evening.

Lady Eva Tudor

Whilst staying with us Chinkie often took off on painting expeditions and travelled by bus all over Wales. We would take her to the nearest suitable bus stop, and she would 'phone when, after a few days or even a week, she needed collecting.

One day she said, "When are you going to take me to Abergenny, Harry?"

"It's pronounced 'Abergavenny' round here Mummy."

"Nonsense. It's always been pronounced 'Abergenny'. I used to know him when I was a girl: Lord Abergenny."

"You'd better learn to say 'Abergavenny' or you'll get lost," replied her son.

All Harry's three sisters came to stay. Margaret and Helen, the two unmarried ones, often arrived with their mother. She used to get their names muddled up and so addressed them both as 'Ma-Helen'. Elizabeth, the eldest daughter, came separately with her husband and two young sons.

It was while Helen was staying with us that the swarm of bees arrived from nowhere. I noticed it hanging from a low branch of one of the apple trees, but had no idea what to do about it, or even if there was anyone living locally who kept bees.

"Do you know anything about bees, Helen?" I asked hopefully.

"Oh yes," said Helen, who was an expert on many diverse matters. "All we have to do is borrow a 'skep' (I think that was the word) and take the swarm. It's quite easy."

I consulted a villager who said he knew someone who would lend us a skep, and he went off to borrow it.

"Now," Helen instructed me, "We must put on large hats, veils and bee-proof clothing and gloves. "Have you got a hat with a wide brim?"

I could not at first think of one, but then remembered the R.A.F. solar topee I had been equipped with during the war. This I gave to Helen and she covered it, her face and neck with a veil of butter muslin.

The amateur beekeepers

As for me, having no more suitable hats, I wore an inverted Italian fruit basket, also swathed in muslin. We protected the rest of our bodies in tightly buttoned coats (I wore mine back to front for extra safety), wellies and large gardening gloves. Then Helen carefully shook the brown, quivering mass into the skep. Success! A proper modern bee-hive was now an urgent necessity and was bought that very afternoon. That was how I became an amateur beekeeper.

The following day the man who had lent us the skep came to retrieve it and to inspect the bees who were busily settling into their immaculate new home. He puffed away silently at his pipe.

"I hope they're not Eyetalians," he said at last, gloomily.

"Why? What's wrong with Eyetalians?" I politely pronounced the word the same way as he had done.

"Oh, it's nasty they are. Bad-tempered, you know."

"How can you tell if they are Eyetalians?"

"Well," he said, "They look much darker-like than English bees."

That seemed natural enough. Two bees taxied out of the hive and took off without delay. They did look rather dark and swarthy. Quite clearly a couple of Mediterranean individuals.

After the bee-keeping expert had gone, I stayed beside the hive for a while listening to the soft, busy humming inside. What were they singing? *On with the Motley? Come back to Sorrento? Funiculi, funicula?* Or perhaps *The Flight of the Beedle Bum?* I hoped it was none of these but something placid and gentle like, *In an English Country Garden.*

Now I had to buy a further 'How to' book: this time called *All You Need To Know About Bee-Keeping.* I had hoped the bees might keep us - in honey anyhow - for now we had all three, the Land, the Milk and the Honey. But although we had those bees for two years, there was very little honey to spare for us. The reason may have been two consecutive bad summers.

When winter approached we were entitled to a special ration of sugar to be made into a syrup to supplement the bees' honey stores. I was very tempted to use the sugar for human consumption, as our ration was still very small. But I did not, and the syrup was poured into the appropriate section at the top of the hive and helped to keep the bees alive.

Then one summer day while doing something quite clever and technical with 'supers', I was stung on the leg. It had often happened before but this time my leg blew up like a barrage balloon and huge water blisters formed on top of the skin. I was feeling very peculiar too, so Harry popped me into the car and drove me to our doctor in Ross-on-Wye. After giving me an instant injection, the doctor told me I had become allergic to bee stings and that it would be dangerous for me to be stung again. So the bees and hive were sold as a going concern, and that was the end of my bee-keeping days.

Nine
The Army That Marched On Its Stomach

Now we were obliged to move from the fourteenth century into the twentieth. Dear old Poppy, always so willing, and the primitive farm implements, could not cope with the crops we had to grow. So we bought two tractors, a large blue Fordson and a little grey Ferguson, plus modern implements to be used with them. This meant we also needed some hired help, and we found this immediately in Broad Oak village.

First there was Jack. He was a typically small, dark, stocky Welshman. Even though Broad Oak was in Herefordshire, nearly all the local residents were Welsh. It was a help that our surname was 'Tudor', so though plainly ignorant and inexperienced, we were not considered to be 'foreigners'. Jack's wife was also short in stature, and they lived in a former toll-house, near the Broad Oak Inn. Their house was a minuscule dwelling, with just one completely circular room downstairs, another exactly similar above it and a back kitchen tacked on to the side. Mrs. Jack was called Flossie. It was she who organised the troop of 'girls' who came, first to plant the potatoes, and later to pick them.

With them in the small, round house, lived their young son, and to complete the family, the dog Nellie. She had to be miniature too, to match, and was almost a spaniel, though with a long tail. It was as well Nellie was petite, because whenever she had puppies, which was whenever possible, she had them in a hole in the trunk of the old original 'broad oak'. The tree was now only about ten feet high and almost completely hollow, but it was still just alive, and a few twigs with leaves sprouted every year.

Both Jack and Flossie found it convenient living so close to the inn, so there were mornings when Jack just did not turn up for work and had to sleep off a hangover. As he explained to Harry one day, "When I'm late, I don't come." But being normally such an excellent worker, this was accepted as a reasonable explanation.

The other farm-hand was Joe, a large, gangling youth of sixteen, who already thought he knew everything. A little later when Joe left us, he was replaced for a while by a prisoner-of-war farm worker called Krupa. We never knew his other name. Krupa was another small man, and just as strong as Jack. He always wore a strange pointed felt hat and looked like a cheerful gnome. He spoke little English. Harry spoke no Ukrainian, but they both knew some German. So they communicated with each other in this language. When I think of Krupa nowadays, I always remember the first time I saw his Ukrainian haycocks. It was on a warm June night, still almost as light as day because of the full moon. At 11 p.m. we decided to go down to see what Krupa had been doing with the hay in one of the bottom meadows. An amazing sight met our eyes. English haycocks were usually quite small, but Krupa had transformed that hayfield into a Red Indian encampment. Each haycock was hollow and arranged round a high pole, and to me they looked like rows of wigwams. Harry remembers them as more resembling igloos, so his eyes saw an Esquimo village. But however we viewed them they were magnificent.

As soon as we had settled in, we received instructions from the War Ag. about which crops we were to grow, as some were compulsory and some optional. Potatoes were compulsory and linseed and field beans optional, quite apart from the usual oats, wheat, barley, mangolds and kale and other crops. The field of linseed we grew that first year looked like a deep blue sea when it was in bloom, and the scent of the field beans, when they too were in flower, was unforgettable.

The linseed was harvested and made into a stack to await the arrival of the threshing machine in winter. But one day Guy thought he would have a little bonfire up on the triangular piece of grass near the road, where the stacks stood. Tidy things up a bit. The wind was blowing away from the stacks, so it would be quite safe. Unfortunately the wind veered and a spark blew into the linseed. This was enough to set the old dry stalks and oily seed alight, and soon the stack was ablaze. We still had no mains water and, after Guy had 'phoned for the fire brigade, it was all hands to the pump. Or at least one person pumping like mad, while others careered up and down the drive with buckets of water.

But all our efforts were as just a drop in the ocean, when what we really needed was a flood. The brigade arrived with clanging bells and did their best to dowse the flames with water from a pond. It was too late, but luckily the other stacks did not catch fire.

We had great trouble with a suspicious insurance company after this misadventure. How dare they imagine we would deliberately set fire to our treasured first crop of linseed!

Savoy cabbages were another crop the War Ag. required us to grow. Bundles of young plants were purchased and planted evenly and firmly by a cabbage-planting machine. Once in the ground they were fair game for many different types of predator. We discovered this the hard way. During their short lives they were attacked by at least seven adversaries, rather like the Plagues of Egypt.

To give them a good start, their baby roots had first to be dipped in calomel to protect them from the dreaded 'club-root'.

Then they endured trial by drought. This caused them to droop and hang their heads like old men with bent backs. We feared they would never straighten. Mercifully when they had been reduced to almost lying flat, it rained for several days, and gradually they stood upright and looked proud. We heaved a sigh of relief.

The third plague followed immediately. Unknown to us thousands of voracious slugs and snails had been waiting for months, or even years, in the long grass and debris beneath the field hedges, for just this day.

Guy came in to breakfast looking pale and anguished and sounding incoherent.

"The savoys!" he gasped. "Come on! Come on! Now!"

We followed him to the savoy field. The first six feet of little cabbage plants had been totally demolished. All that remained were a few small pieces of stalk and the slimy trails of slugs and snails returning, satiated, to the undergrowth. There could be no doubt about the culprits.

We had to act quickly: the army of gastropods would return the following night and devour another six-foot width of plants. The car sped to S.H.A.C.S. (South Herefordshire Agricultural Co-Operative Society) in Ross-on-Wye. Huge bags of slug killer were purchased, and a thick defensive layer of the deadly stuff spread round the remaining savoy plants. We reckoned that before they reached the next rows of cabbages, our slimy enemies would be forced to slither through the slug killer. Would they be able to abstain from eating it?

Next morning Guy had a satisfied smile on his face at breakfast.

"Come and look at the savoys *now!*" he said once again. They looked exactly as they had the previous day; there were no more casualties. But surrounding them was a sea of slugs and snails of every shape, size and colour, all now dead and dehydrating into stiff shapes in the hot sun. It was a revolting but, in the circumstances, most pleasing sight. Whatever lethal ingredient the slug killer contained it was completely irresistible to all gastropods.

I had not given much thought to slugs and so on until this incident. They were just a nuisance in the garden, but could easily be trapped under half an orange or grapefruit skin. Now I wanted to know more. An encyclopaedic book about wildlife was full of information.

I discovered many fascinating facts about slugs. That slugs and snails are really the same animal, although the snail looks tidier and more attractive, as it covers its nasty slimy parts with a neat, colourful shell. That they are rapacious eaters - this we knew already, only too well -

have two pairs of retractable tentacles, smell through one pair and have eyes on the tips of the second pair. Biologically hermaphrodites, they have peculiar and most unusual mating habits, which I am not going to describe. The book suggested that if a surplus of gastropods was available, we could try eating them. Snail and slug stew perhaps? No, not for us, with or without garlic!

The cabbages were not out of the wood yet. The news got around to the pigeons that there were succulent young savoys at Caldicott. The birds arrived in flocks and pecked away at the growing leaves. Harry's patent bird scarer was installed in the field and banged away until the pigeons gave up and flew to ravage some other crop elsewhere.

Plague number five was Cabbage White butterflies followed by their green and black caterpillars. We did another panic run to S.H.A.C.S. to buy anti-caterpillar spray. Harry and Guy then marched up and down the field with spray containers fixed on their backs. The caterpillars stopped munching and crashed to the ground.

Towards the end of that summer a plague of aphids descended on the now almost-mature savoys. The outer leaves turned yellow and started to wilt. But another spraying session with an anti-aphid spray dealt with them.

By autumn the cabbages had survived six plagues and were looking fat and prosperous, just ready for cutting. They would now have to endure the seventh and final plague which would at last finish them off: a plague of human cabbage cutters this time. "Savoys are at their best if cut after the first frost," the experts instructed. We waited till the weather was bitterly cold and the cabbages covered with rime. Then, wearing sacks on our backs for warmth, more sacks round our waists for protection, mittens on frozen hands and armed with sharp knives, we slowly walked the field decapitating each cabbage and throwing it into a net bag. The savoys had been harvested.

The War Ag. demanded potatoes as well, and many farmers grumbled about being compelled to grow this crop. It was here that Flossie and her efficient team of 'girls' of all ages first showed their prowess. Potatoes were planted by a potato-planting machine operated by a human being who sat in a very uncomfortable seat on the back.

Some previous summer she had gone on an outing to Barry Island. There she had bought a comical souvenir. It was a kind of Victorian poke-bonnet with 'kiss-me-quick' written across the front. Flossie was very attached to this hat. She always wore it when the girls came back in the late summer to pick the potatoes after the rows had been ploughed up by the tractor. Nobody liked this back-breaking work, but it was not a purely feminine job. Men worked as potato pickers too, but I could not help noticing how much quicker the girls were filling the sacks. I think it was because they picked up the potatoes while bending their knees, whereas the men merely bent their backs. Perhaps women have more flexible knees?

Ten
Culture Comes To Caldicott

After about eighteen months working together as a threesome, Guy decided it was time to leave us to either sink or swim. He would now float away on his own. Harry and I were very grateful for all his help and instruction. The three of us had learnt a lot during those months, much of it by making painful mistakes.

Each of the animal sections had expanded greatly. In the Cattle Command the initial baby bull calves had grown into young bullocks. Some had gone to market, others were still with us, being fattened as store cattle, and all had been replaced by yet more little bull calves.

The Pig Platoon was very much larger, and lucky old Howie Dainty Boy had additional lovely young wives living in wooden huts scattered round the orchard by now. He had become dad to countless litters of baby pigs.

My Poultry Patrols had increased at least ten-fold and were becoming overwhelming. People kept on telling me that poultry keeping was a woman's job and that selling eggs and poultry were the farmer's wife's 'perks'. But in our case the poultry section was so big that the perks were not mine. So another volume joined the collection of 'How To .....' books. It was called *How to keep Poultry and Make a Profit*. I found the title a little discouraging. It inferred that it was only too easy to keep poultry and make a loss.

Most of my laying hens, reared from day-old chicks, lived in the orchard and were divided into four different tribes. Each tribe had its chief in the form of a bossy rooster, and we placed the henhouses strategically, at least two hundred yards apart, hoping the chiefs would not meet and start tribal warfare.

By now I was also rearing young cockerels for the table. They too arrived as day-old chicks and, when they had outgrown the horrible hover, were put out in the fields in little houses called 'arks'. There they led a happy and carefree life eating lots of lovely fattening food until they were about four months old. But meanwhile they sometimes developed a disease called 'coccidiosis': too disgusting to describe. Luckily there was a cure, a medicine which was mixed with their drinking water so that each time they had a drink they got a dose. A friend who was staying with us came with me on my poultry feeding and watering round one day. She was appalled by what she saw: there was a bad outbreak of coccidiosis amongst the young cockerels at the time.

"Harry! It's really too awful!" she cried when we returned. "All Sonia's chickens have got sicko!"

At the age of four months they were put to the test. By now they were supposed to weigh over four pounds each, and Joe and I would weigh each bird using a small spring balance. It was an undignified process for the adolescent cockerels. Joe would tie their legs together and the loop of twine would be put over the hook of the spring balance. They did not enjoy being weighed while hanging upside down and would squawk in outraged protest. Any bird weighing over four pounds was destined to become a 'young roaster' without delay. He would not live long enough to become a 'young rooster'. Those below this weight were condemned by Joe with the single word, 'opeless.

All the 'opeless ones then went into a kind of open prison where they were stuffed with food but deprived of exercise. This rather drastic treatment led to the outbreak of another dreadful disease; although perhaps it would be more correct to say, it brought out a nasty trait in their characters. It was cannibalism. Apparently this often broke out when poultry were shut up in close proximity to each other. Number one cockerel in the pecking order would start it by pecking at the rump of number two, also plucking out some feathers for the hell of it.

Number two would take it out on number three, who would attack number four and so on down to the smallest and weakest, who would usually end up bloody, minus all feathers and pecked to death.

I was mystified by this revolting and, I considered, unnatural behaviour. As I had by now become an avid reader of *The Poultry World*, I wrote to them for advice. Both my letter and their answer were published. It went something like this.

Dear Mrs. T.,

I am so sorry to hear about your young cockerels. This is quite a common phenomenon among closely confined poultry. It is called 'cannibalism!' The cure is to fit them all with special dark glasses, obtainable from Messrs. So & So at Such & Such address.

Yours truly, etc.

I could just imagine them all walking around looking like American gangsters, but keeping their beaks to themselves. Well they were certainly already behaving like Al Capone and his mob. But one thing puzzled me, how could a cockerel who had no ear lobes keep his spectacles on? It did not seem a very practical idea to me and expensive too, so I let the whole lot out of prison and, with other things to think about, they gave up their vile practice.

At some point Harry noticed I was getting very tired and that my arms had become much longer. This was due to the heavy buckets of water, mixed corn and layers or growers mash I had to carry twice daily all over the farm to the ever-increasing poultry. They were constantly on the move. Harry and Guy had read, learned and inwardly digested the Henderson Brothers book called *Farming, How To Start*. This had become their unofficial Bible. The Hendersons advocated 'folding' poultry over the land to increase its fertility (the land, not the poultry). So every few days the rows of hen-houses and arks were towed a short distance by the tractor. This was too much for their pea-brained inhabitants. When bedtime came they all assembled on the spot where their house had been the previous night, quite incapable of recognising it twenty yards away.

"Where is our house", they cried complainingly.

"Why have they taken it away?"

"It was on this spot yesterday ...."

"Oh well, we'd better settle down here for the night".

So it was decided that I needed a poultry assistant, and we advertised in *The Farmers Weekly* for: "A Strong Girl, no experience needed, etc."

I do not know why we chose Olivia Gloyn. Perhaps she was the only one who answered? She told us she had been working in a large London bookshop and before that had been a policewoman. When she arrived I showed her all the cockerels in far-flung places she would have to visit twice daily and the four tribes living close at hand in the orchard. She literally took a great load off my shoulders

The young pullets had been made very comfortable in their new, clean hen-houses. The nest boxes had been lined with soft hay and a white china egg put in each: a hint of what was required of them. I could remember seeing those pot eggs when I was a little girl and asking my father quite seriously; "Daddy, if a hen sits on a pot egg for three weeks, what does it hatch into?" "A cup and saucer, of course", he had replied. But although I had looked carefully at each hen and accompanying chicks, none seemed to have a cup and saucer on two yellow legs running around with them.

Olivia was also shown where the poultry food was kept in the food store under the granary. Layers mash for the mornings, mixed corn for afternoons and, in a bright yellow packet, the invaluable Karswood poultry spice. This, a very pungent red powder mixed into the warm mash, was another reminder of my father, who had been a great advocate of it as an aid to egg production. "What does Karswood poultry spice do to hens?" I had asked once. "It tickles up their ovaries," he had said. Should I sprinkle a little of this on my morning porridge I had wondered? But no, perhaps not. It might cause me to give birth to quads or quins. Better to let nature take its course.

Olivia was undoubtedly much more cultured than we were. She must have absorbed a lot of information and education while browsing about in the bookshop when it was not busy. She surprised us one day during a meal by suddenly asking, "And what do you think of the Millennium of Hieronymus Bosch?"

"Hieronymus who?"

"Bosch. The Millennium Triptych."

"What is the Millennium … what you've just said?"

"Oh, don't you know?" She looked extremely surprised. "It's a famous painting. I've got a reproduction of it in a book upstairs". She rushed up to her room and returned with a large, flat tome; "Here it is. Isn't it marvellous!"

I studied the picture for a few minutes. So much detail, most of it revolting. So many pale, naked bodies with sad, pained expressions on their faces. Far too many devils wielding forks and evil-looking mythical animals. I found it both nauseating and frightening.

"Sorry Olivia, I'm afraid I think it's gruesome. But then I'm neither as well educated nor as artistic as you are".

Then, some weeks after Olivia's arrival, her 'follower' turned up: a young man with long, unkempt hair, rimless glasses and a wispy beard. 'Hippies' had not happened yet, so Harry dubbed him 'artistic' and I thought of him as 'bohemian'. We were kind and hospitable at first and give him free bed and board for a week. But he showed no sign of moving on and was too delicately made to do any farm work.

"You'll have to ask what's-his-name to move on", I told Olivia. "We can't entertain him indefinitely. Perhaps he could stay at the pub?"

He tried the pub for a few days, did not like it much and returned to London. So did Olivia Gloyn.

Eleven
Send No Money For This Lovely Fizz

After Olivia left us, we engaged a herdswoman to take over the care of the cows and calves, and to thus give Harry more time to devote to arable farming. She was an ex-land girl and she wore her uniform of breeches, long woollen knee socks and green pullover. It suited her down to the ground.

"What is your Christian name?" Harry asked her when she arrived.

"It's Inez," she replied.

"Oh, I can't possibly call you that," said Harry. "I shall call you Fizz."

So Fizz she became to us and, so she said, to all the people she came to know after that.

Fizz would tell us fascinating stories about her wartime experiences and about her subsequent employer after the Land Army had been disbanded. He had been a young bachelor farmer and she had left when he got married. Up until then Fizz had been leading an unusually busy life.

"Who used to do the cooking, Fizz?" I asked her.

"I did."

"As well as all that farm work?"

"Yes."

"How on earth did you find time?"

"Well, I just did something quickly in a saucepan."

What could that 'something' have been? Scrambled eggs perhaps? Baked beans, tinned spaghetti? My imagination ran riot. For additional economy of time and effort they could have had a spoon each and eaten it straight out of the saucepan. Think of the saving in washing up. I discovered what the 'something quickly in a saucepan' was later. Fizz said she made macaroni cheese this way and I suppose it is possible.

Fizz with the dogs

Fizz must have soon realised we knew little about farming and were real beginners, and she was very tactful. But one day she remarked to Harry that a *proper* farmer would have done something differently.

"Don't you think I'm a *proper* farmer, Fizz?" Harry sounded rather hurt.

"Of course I do," Fizz assured him. "But you know what I mean..." She was embarrassed and her voice trailed away.

I knew what she meant. Harry was not an improper farmer, but he was not a born and bred one. And I was not a *proper* farmer's wife. I did not wear a flowered smock or pinny to start with. I wore comfortable and practical bib-and-brace dungarees. Mine were now quite eye-catching. I had just found a shop, via the small ads in a newspaper, that sold them in red, blue, yellow and green, as well as the usual beige.

I have not yet described any of our numerous farm cats. Their tale is told in chapter fifteen, but at this point I must mention the large, handsome ex-tomcat called Tarzan, who was absolutely devoted to Fizz. He had been one of Tiger's kittens and Tiger was our first cat.

At evening meals sitting round our makeshift dining table in the hall, Tarzan always settled himself on Fizz's lap. He looked benevolent, self-satisfied and somnolent, but in spite of his half-shut eyes, he was far from asleep. Whenever Fizz's attention was distracted for a second, a large, grey paw would scoop a tasty morsel off her plate onto her lap, and Tarzan would swallow it.

Fizz's bedroom was over the dairy and her window looked out onto the sloping roof. At night-time, after a successful hunting session, Tarzan would make his way via the roof into Fizz's room, often bringing her a present. Sometimes it was half a rat, sometimes half a rabbit. She became quite accustomed to waking with Tarzan asleep on her stomach, and his grisly gift laid beside her on the pillow. But one night he excelled himself and brought her a small, live rabbit.

Fizz was apt to oversleep and that morning when Harry knocked on her door to wake her, she opened it and thrust a squirming little rabbit into his hands. "Here, take this!" she said.

It was a double surprise for Harry: first the rabbit and second the unexpected vision of a nude Fizz.

Like us she became a keen theatregoer. In spite of our busy working day we did find time to go to the theatre in Hereford. It was not the beautiful new building they have in that cathedral city now, but the small repertory theatre, known as the 'County', tucked away in a side street near the cathedral. It was always a rush to get there before the curtain rose, and if we had not had time for supper we would telephone and ask them to make us some sandwiches, which they would do most obligingly. At other times we grabbed some kind of food and ate it in the car while driving in. Fizz, sitting alone on the back seat, would hand round the rations. I can remember her hungrily gnawing pieces of chicken in her fingers and then nonchalantly tossing the bones out of the car window. It must have been a side-effect from consorting with someone called Henry Tudor. She had obviously at some time seen Charles Laughton in *The Private Life of Henry VIII*.

Once at the theatre we usually saw a performance by the repertory company. But every now and then there would be a treat in the form of a touring company. We saw the Young Vic performing *Macbeth* which brought back memories to me of School Certificate, for which I seemed to have had to analyse every word and punctuation mark of 'The Scottish Play'. There was one extraordinarily funny ballet company. They were not intentionally funny, but on the contrary, deadly, deadpan serious. The small stage was not constructed for people to leap around on and it bounced with them. When some hefty but scantily clad girls crashed onto it and started doing *The Dance of the Little Swans* Harry whispered to me, "They look as if they're saying 'Oh dear! We've all lost our bath towels!'"

After them a small, but beautifully formed, little man, bursting out of his costume, pranced around, apparently dancing a *pas de deux* with a rose, which he alternately tossed in the air or wept over. I imagine this must have been *The Spectre of the Rose* and we should have taken him more seriously and not laughed so much.

There was just one very small thing that Harry did not approve of about Fizz. It was her copious use of wintergreen ointment. She suffered from aches and strains, as we all did, and her favourite remedy for this was wintergreen. Harry could not stand its pungent aroma. I did not mind it at all. It did not smell any worse than the Elliman's embrocation we used on our own minor injuries. There were two types of Elliman's. One was for use by humans and the other to be used on horses. Years earlier someone had once told me that the horse version was much the stronger and worked even faster. So we anointed our sprains and bruises with this powerful stuff, which although it removed at least one layer of skin *en route*, soon got to the seat of the trouble.

Many other patent panaceas for day-to-day accidents and mishaps appeared at weekends in national newspapers. On Saturdays and Sundays most newspapers devoted at least two full pages to small ads. Each of these measured only two to three inches square, but this was enough space for some pithy description and usually an illustration as well.

I had my favourites. 'Top of the Pops' for me was one showing a frightened-looking man holding up his hands in horror. Out of his mouth appeared a bubble containing the words: "No truss for me!" One assumed someone was walking towards him holding out a truss in a menacing manner.

I was fond too, of a longer advertisement which showed an earnest man wearing a kindly look and spectacles. He was pointing a finger directly at the reader in Field Marshal Kitchener style, not saying: 'Your Country Needs You', but 'Let me be your father'. It seemed he was advertising correspondence courses, but if he really wanted to be my father, should he not have done something about it much, much earlier?

It appeared also from the weekend small ads that it was perfectly possible to clothe yourself from head to foot without spending a penny. 'Send no money for this lovely skirt', said one advertisement, 'Send no money for these sturdy shoes', said another, 'Send no money for these smart trousers, warm shirts and fashionable coats etc.' And under all these desirable, apparently free garments, one could wear the alternative to a truss - whatever that might be. There must have been a catch somewhere, but as we never ordered any of these 'free' offers, we did not find out what it was.

In the meantime Fizz, sadly for us, had fallen in love with a medical student at Hereford Hospital. Her interests now veered towards caring for sick people, rather than cows. So she opted to take a nursing course at the same hospital. We were very sorry to lose such a friendly, compatible helper, but Fizz, I am glad to say, returned into our lives several years later.

Twelve
Living off the Land

By now the ever-expanding poultry section was starting to make a profit. The point-of-lay pullets came to the point at last and laid. Their first offerings were tiny, not much larger than pigeons' eggs, but they grew steadily larger and we had to send them weekly to the egg packing station. This created another most monotonous and boring chore: rubbing the eggs clean, or even, most illegally, actually washing them. They had to be in pristine condition to be worthy of the 'little lion', hallmark of the British egg, stamped on them. Some hens, although provided with comfortable, clean nesting boxes, were careless, so this was not my favourite job, and one I often put off till the last possible moment, just before the egg van was due to arrive.

Other vans came to collect the table birds and very occasionally we ate a chicken ourselves. But I knew well that 'any profit must be ploughed back into the farm' and turned into more livestock or machinery. That was one of Harry's rules. Ploughing back anything into the farm house was not encouraged. If we made a habit of eating young chickens we would be eating our profits.

So we concentrated instead on the far too plentiful wild rabbits. I tried every possible rabbit recipe I could find and invented several of my own. Rabbit stew, casserole or pie were every day fare. But with a little more ingenuity I could concoct *fricassée* of rabbit, curried rabbit, rabbit goulash, *blanquette de lapin*, rabbit *à la* king and rabbit mousse. This last one was so delectable you could not detect rabbit in it at all. It tasted like finely minced spring chicken extravagantly combined with cream and herbs.

Once or twice we were given a piece of venison from Cwm Madoc. They waged unceasing war against the deer in Nant-y-Wain wood, who leapt over fences and ate their young crops. I had never cooked venison before, and the first time Gordon Williams, the number two son, brought the meat to us, he also brought the recipe of how to cook it, from his stepmother. I was to first make a thick flour and water paste, like pastry but minus the fat. The venison was to be wrapped in this and then cooked. It sounded a surprising method to my uninformed mind, but it worked.

Then there was the red letter day when Harry's friend 'V.G.' got his 'right and left', while walking round the farm with his gun: a cock pheasant with the right barrel and a rabbit with the left. The eagle-eyed marksman was congratulated and we all had an unexpected tasty meal after the pheasant had been hung for a few days. "Leave them to hang till their tails drop off," my father had always advised, but I thought that was going a bit too far.

A hare was shot one day and brought into the kitchen by Harry. "Here's something different for the pot," he said. Hoo-ray! I had always loved jugged hare, but had never actually jugged one myself. This hare still had its coat on, but that should not present any difficulty; I had skinned hundreds of rabbits by now. However there was a very noticeable difference. I discovered that a hare is the bloodiest animal possible, in the literal sense of the word. It was a horrible task and one I would think twice about before doing again.

We were not very self-sufficient in fruit, although our plums were good. Seven or eight Victoria plum trees grew between the kitchen garden and the new Dutch barn, and these fruited prolifically most years. But in the orchard the remaining apple and pear trees were old, gnarled and covered with lichen. They had some blossom each year but the resulting fruit was, like the trees, dry, wrinkled and cracked. We discovered why the pears were small, hard and quite inedible. They were perry pears, so perhaps the apples had been cider apples in their day. There was just one tree that almost every year produced a bountiful crop of crisp, sweet, juicy apples, so we harvested every one.

"What do you call these apples, Jack?" I asked him.

"Why, they's Broad Eyes Tired".

"What?"

"Broad Eyes Tired," he said in a louder voice.

"Oh."

I told Harry what Jack had said about the apples. "Would you ask Jack their name, please? I don't think he and I are talking the same language."

Harry did. "Jack says they're called Broad Eyes Tired", he said. We gave up.

Mushrooms abounded in the late summer and autumn in one particular field. The residents of Broad Oak knew they were there too, and if I wanted mushrooms I had to get up even earlier in the morning than they did. Mushrooms were free for all in the country, rather like blackberries. But one source of free food had been overlooked. I had noticed curious white or yellowish globular shapes growing in the orchard grass. They were obviously fungi of some kind, but I had been taught to distrust all fungi except mushrooms. If I could find these other strange round fungi at the psychological moment when they had attained their full size, had turned brown but had not yet started to wrinkle, I could stamp on them with most satisfying results. Clouds of dark smoke would spout into the air as if someone had just dropped a small bomb, scattering spores far and wide. I took a childish delight in doing this.

Gordon noticed me stamping around in the orchard one day.

"Why are you squashing those puff-balls?" he asked.

"Just for fun."

"Don't you know you can eat them?"

"Can you really, Gordon? I thought they were poisonous."

"No, they're lovely sliced and fried in butter with a bit of bacon and egg. Look, you want to pick them when they're this size," and he picked several plump white things resembling golf balls.

Next day I added them to the menu for breakfast.

"What's for breakfast today?" asked Harry, seeing me busy with the frying pan.

"Fried eggs and puff-balls."

"But they're poisonous!" Harry exclaimed. "Don't give *me* any."

"Not for me either, thank you," said Fizz quickly.

"Gordon says they're delicious cooked in butter," I told them, piling the whole lot onto my plate. "If I'm dead tomorrow, you're right - if I'm alive, you're wrong!"

I lived.

It was while browsing through a country cookbook for new ways to cook rabbit that I met the recipe for elderflower wine. It sounded so simple that I was sure even a complete nitwit could succeed. Before this the nearest I had ever come to making home-made wine was when my father and I made sloe gin. It was just after I had left school when we lived in the country. The blackthorn was heavy with sloes that year, but they tasted bitter and set my teeth on edge. "Let's make sloe gin," suggested my father. "It's very easy. All you need are sloes, sugar, lots of gin and some long darning needles." Gin, at that time, cost only 12/6 a bottle – 62½p in modern currency. Whisky cost the same. My father said that when he was young, whisky was only 3/6 a bottle.

So, each armed with a sharp darning needle, we proceeded to pierce every sloe twice, once in the top and once in the bottom, and then half filled empty bottles with the fruit. Some sugar was added and finally each bottle was filled to the top with gin and firmly corked. We were then supposed to leave it severely alone for three to six months. It was difficult to forget the maturing sloe gin, so every week or so we had a taste to see how it was progressing. As time passed it grew nicer and nicer until at last the great day came when it was officially mature and ready for consumption. But by this time there was not a great deal of actual sloe gin left, just a lot of alcoholic sloes which we ate with teaspoons one day, instead of a pudding.

For the elderflower wine, I had to pick heads of elderflower at the precise moment they were in full bloom and preferably when the sun was shining on them. They smelt deliciously of grapes.

"Now," said the recipe, "put the elderflower blossoms in a preserving pan with rinds and juice of oranges and lemons. Add a gallon of boiling water and let the mixture boil for half an hour."

This treatment had a most disastrous effect on the flowers.

"Are you cooking a cat?" asked Harry as he passed through the kitchen and saw me stirring something in the pan.

"No, I'm not! I exclaimed indignantly. "I'm making elderflower wine."

"Well, don't expect me to drink it," he said, carefully shutting the kitchen door to keep the dreadful smell out of the rest of the house.

He was right. It did smell exactly like tom-cat, but I carried on. After this stage, sugar was added and, when the revolting mixture was luke-warm, one ounce of yeast spread on a piece of toast - I have never forgotten that 'piece of toast' - was left floating on the surface to start fermentation. But after this most unpromising beginning the nauseous brew miraculously turned into a delicious, grape-like, white wine. "Leave for six months before drinking", the recipe commanded. Once again, by the time six months had elapsed, during which we had tasted it many times, there was little left. After repeating the process the following year, I hid the bottles in an inaccessible place for six months. During this time it was transformed into a nectar which with age became increasingly, and dangerously, alcoholic.

Thirteen
Murder in the Old Orchard

And now I have to tell you the true but sad story of the Chief of the Red Leg tribe. I have already mentioned him once, as he was our first cockerel and arrived with the initial batch of point-of-lay pullets.

The Red Leg pullet squaws and their chief lived in the orchard together with the other three tribes and their accompanying chiefs. The Red Legs occupied the nearest hen house to the food store, so they were more privileged and got fed and watered first every morning and afternoon. I looked after them tenderly and efficiently, as I did all my poultry.

But as the Red Legs' chief grew older, he became more and more belligerent, and we christened him Monty, as that seemed an appropriate name. With advancing age, the sharp spurs on the backs of his legs grew longer and more pointed and he developed a great antipathy towards me, his benefactor and protector. After I had fed Monty and his squaws, I had to pass through his territory three times on my way to feed the other tribes. I carried a bucket of water in one hand and another of layers mash or mixed corn in the other. Monty guarded his territory jealously. Arrayed in beautiful green and red feathers, he would observe me inscrutably from his vantage point a little higher up the slope. He made me feel like a pioneer in a covered wagon, trekking west through Indian country. Then he would suddenly take off in my direction, neck and wings outstretched, and comb and wattles purple with fury, sometimes running and sometimes flying for a short distance.

After his first vicious attack on my legs I was usually ready for him and would throw the contents of the water bucket in his face, followed by the bucket itself. But this, of course, meant another walk back to the tap to replace the water. I would return with a further bucketful, but armed this time with the yard brush, which had a stiff, spiky head. Troublesome roosters hated this weapon. As Corporal Jones used to remark in *Dad's Army*, "They don't like it up 'em!" So, feeding the laying hens had become a protracted job. Buckets of water were flung at Monty for several months, but he continued his hostile attacks. We both became increasingly infuriated and the situation developed into a war to the death. It was going to be HIM or ME!

One day, having at last succeeded in getting food and water to everybody in the orchard, I walked back swinging two empty buckets. Something on the ground caught my eye. I bent to pick it up, and as I did so, a heavy weight thudded on to my left arm and two sharp spurs ripped through my jacket and straight into my flesh. I could see blood pouring from two wounds, but my dander was up by then. I hurled empty buckets and invective at Monty and chased him back to his H.Q. I was spitting mad.

"I'll get you, you beastly bird!" I shouted, "Just wait till tonight, THEN you'll find what's coming to you. Yes, wait till tonight!"

Then I walked, backwards for safety, to the food store.

When dusk had fallen, I went as usual to shut all the popholes of the various poultry houses and I visited Monty's house last. But this time I carried a powerful torch.

By the way, did you know that hens sing songs before they go to sleep? We had often heard them at it, with the rooster in charge as the conductor. Our hens seemed to favour Elizabethan madrigals and anything containing lots of 'Hey nonny no's.' Each hen sang her part perfectly, joining in the round at precisely the right moment.

That night Monty, on his rostrum, was conducting as usual and the choir girls were sitting on their perches with their heads raised in song. I shut the pophole, then I opened the door of the hen house, went in and closed it carefully behind me. I switched on the torch and shone it directly on to Monty. While he was blinded and surprised by this sudden bright light, I seized the chance to grab him by the legs. He felt as heavy as a full bucket of corn as I carried him out into the twilit orchard.

Loud squawks of, "Help! Kidnap! Murder! Fire! Foxes! Send for the police!" came from his wives, and the other tribes added to the clamour from their houses, shrieking, screeching and cackling in sympathy. I took no notice, being entirely preoccupied by the problem of getting my fingers round his neck in the correct dislocating position, without getting pecked to pieces. When I did, I found his neck much thicker, tougher and more sinewy than that of the average hen or young cockerel. That deft jerk, taught me by my father, did not work on him. Meanwhile he was flapping his great wings about like a demented windmill.

I began to panic, realising there was now no alternative but strangulation, so I twisted his long, muscular neck round and round and round like a corkscrew. He took a long, frightening time to die, but at length his eyes glazed over, and when I released my grip, his neck untwisted itself and hung motionless. The only movement was an occasional nervous twitch from his wings.

Full of triumph, I carried him into the scullery and laid him on the floor. But now that the dreadful deed had been done, I was beginning to feel like Lady Macbeth and, glancing at my hands, saw they were indeed covered with blood from his poor ruptured neck. I washed them several times, muttering, "Out, damned spot," as I did so. Then I looked again at Monty, inert on the floor. His head lay in a large pool of blood.

"Who'd have thought the old rooster would have so much blood in him?" I marvelled.

Further reaction had set in by now, and with very mixed feelings I sought out Harry, who was in the sitting room, listening to the radio.

"You've been a long time," he said, "Have you had a problem?"

"Yes and no," I replied, "I think I've solved one problem and created another. Harry, could you find time to take me into either Ross or Hereford tomorrow? It's rather urgent."

"What is it that you need so urgently?" he asked.

"Well, I shall have to buy a very, very, large saucepan indeed."

Fourteen
Neighbours

All through that first summer at Caldicott every farming process was new to us. And, so soon after the end of the war, much farming was still done by hand.

We ploughed the fields and scattered. At least Guy ploughed using the tractor and Harry scattered. He was even shown how to sow by 'broadcasting' seed out of a bag, walking systematically up and down a field throwing seed first to the right and then to the left. The method had not changed since Biblical times. I did not understand why the field could not be planted in the usual way using a seed drill pulled either by Poppy or the tractor. There must have been a very good reason.

The corn was cut with a reaper and binder in the good old-fashioned way, and we learned how to stook it in neat rows - six sheaves to each stook - so that the corn and straw could finish drying before being carried in on wagons to be stacked. The whole procedure was very picturesque and, viewed from a slightly higher point, the fields of stooked corn looked as if they had been smocked by some expert needlewoman. Stooking was hard on the hands because our corn, that year, contained a lot of thistles. It was also advisable, we found, to wear a long-sleeved shirt as the spiky straw scratched our arms.

Gathering in the corn was not all sun bonnets and flowing skirts as depicted in idyllic pictures of harvesters.

After the first harvest came the first winter and our introduction to the threshing machine. It was then we realised how essential it was to have friendly neighbours.

The Williams family at Cwm Madoc have been described already, but there were two more farms on our boundaries. To the north was 'Evans the Moor' and to the east 'Evans the Hill'.

Map of Caldicott Farm showing neighbouring farms

Having an imaginative mind I pictured Evans the Moor as a dark-skinned man of Moroccan blood, with at least four wives, all wearing yashmaks. But, disappointingly, he was not, and there was only one Mrs. Evans the Moor.

As for Evans the Hill, he should more accurately have been called 'Evans the Rabbits'. It was true he lived on a hill as we did, and our two farms faced each other. The little brook which emerged from Nant-y-Wain wood, and ran between the two farms, was our joint boundary. We could see his farmhouse and the vast, single grass field that ran down hill from it. He never grew any crop there, for it was a honeycomb of rabbit warrens. Thousands of little, grey bodies with white scuts hopped around on the short turf, and it did not seem to worry him a bit. He may have been selling rabbits to butchers, as the weekly meat ration was still very small. But we found the hungry bunnies a bit of a menace. They could easily either leap across or swim the brook, and it became necessary to dig in wire netting quite deeply along the boundary to stop them eating all our crops.

Guy said we would need extra help when the threshing machine came that winter, and that if we borrowed one man from each of our farming neighbours, Cwm Madoc, The Moor and The Hill, we could cope. The threshing machine arrived at 4 a.m. one morning so that the great steam traction engine which powered both the thresher and baler could get up steam before the work had to start. The traction engine thundered down the road at this unsocial hour making an ear-splitting clattering noise and towing the thresher and baler behind it. It must have woken up the whole village.

The plan was to make an early start. In my innocence and ignorance, I thought the farmer's wife's only job that day would be to make gallons of tea and serve some sort of meal to the threshing crew and neighbouring helpers. So I was hanging around watching the preliminary preparations with great interest. It would have been wiser to have hidden instead. Guy counted up the available help and found he had miscalculated. He was one short. "You'll have to help," he said to me.

"What! Me?" I exclaimed.

"Yes, you. Get up onto the top of the threshing drum and cut the bands of baler twine around each sheaf," Guy said, handing me a knife.

I clambered up and the drum beneath my feet started to throb and shake. Jack tossed a sheaf down to me from the top of the stack.

"Cut the twine," instructed Guy, "and hand the sheaf to Joe. And, for Heaven's sake, don't cut your hand off or throw yourself into the drum."

This was to be the pattern of my actions for what seemed an age. The machine hummed away, an insatiable, unstoppable monster. We rapidly became smothered in dark grit and dust, which caked our clothes, faces and hair, and entered our eyes, noses and throats. Down below, others took the full sacks of corn from the machine, tied them up and wheeled them away. The straw was ejected from the top of the other end of the drum and was pitched into the baler, from which it emerged as neat, rectangular, twine-bound parcels. I wondered how long this torment would last before we had a break.

Suddenly there was a shout of "Bait time!" I had been told this was my cue to produce large quantities of tea for the thirsty men to drink with their 'bait' of bread and cheese. To be truthful I cannot remember who made the tea that day. Was it me? Probably. Much too soon the great monster started to quiver and groan again, and I resumed my position on the drum. We were off once more.

While standing there catching, cutting and throwing, a thought occurred to me. Hell must be something like this: heat, dust and noise, full of people wielding pitchforks.

Several hours later there was another shout: "Dinner time!" The machine stopped and here was my second cue: to feed the threshing crew this time. Luckily I had put an enormous stew and a vast rice pudding in a slow oven earlier that morning, determined not to be caught out.

After dinner we returned to our positions, and I noticed that each man had string tied round the bottom of his trousers.

"Why have you all tied up your trouser legs?" I asked Jack.

"Rats," Jack replied briefly. "We'll come to them at the bottom of the stack. You'd better do the same missus," he said, tossing me two lengths of string.

Horrified, I obeyed, tying the string so tightly I almost cut off the circulation of blood to my feet. But mercifully nothing lasts forever. It was over. The last sheaf, the last trickle of corn and the last blast of chaff had been processed by the machine. We were all very tired and looked like a dissipated troupe of black and white minstrels with our black faces and hands, and blood-shot eyes.

I was also, probably unjustifiably, very cross and angry. I confronted Guy: "Look here," I said. "I can be either Mrs. Jekyll the farmer's wife, doling out food and drink to the threshing crew, or I can be tough Mrs. Hyde, cutting twine on top of the drum. But I can't be both simultaneously. Never ask me to do this again."

Guy was just as tired, and took it well. "O.K.," he said, "I'm very sorry about today. Next year we'll be better organised."

So far I have only mentioned farming neighbours, but we did have some other non-farming friends. About two miles down the road towards Monmouth was Pembridge Castle, a very old stronghold, one of a line of English castles defending the country from the invading wild hordes in the Welsh Marches. The castle was owned by an elderly couple who lived in part of it. The farmer cultivating the surrounding land occupied another part, and the remainder was empty and disintegrating.

I cannot now remember their names, so I shall refer to them as the Old Gentleman and the Old Lady. The Old Gentleman was tall and angular, and reminded me somehow of George Bernard Shaw. It was not because he had either red hair or a beard, so it must have been his style of dress: the tweed Norfolk jacket, knickerbockers and long socks with turn-over tops. And, I imagined, G.B.S. would have been just as garrulous as he was. The Old Lady, by contrast, was small, quiet and self-effacing. She was a demure pea-hen to his strutting peacock.

The Old Gentleman had lived a very full life, if all he told us was to be believed. First, he said, he had had a long career as a surgeon, and had performed the very first appendectomy operation. This must have been in the early 1900's, although he did not claim that his patient was King Edward VII. Then, at about age of fifty, he had changed horses, read law, passed all his exams and become a successful lawyer. Wearying of this second career after a while he had then studied the Greek Orthodox Church, and in due course emerged as a fully qualified Greek Orthodox priest. And now, he told us, he was a bishop.

This dear old couple often walked over to see us to have a cup of tea, taking a short cut across the fields. On one occasion we told him that Chinkie and Harry's second sister, Margaret, were coming to stay the following day.

"Margaret Tudor coming to stay here?" he cried excitedly. "Why, the ghost of Margaret Tudor haunts my chapel! I've often seen her there. You must bring them both over to tea with us."

Why was Margaret Tudor lurking in his chapel, I wondered? All I could remember about her was that she had been the eldest daughter of the Henry Tudor who became Henry VII, and that she had married James IV of Scotland. But what possible connection could she have had with Pembridge Castle?" I consulted a history book and found that Henry VII had been born in Pembroke Castle, but that is a different place. It remained a mystery to me.

So one afternoon we all went to tea at the castle, taking the same short cut across the fields. Harry and I had been inside the castle quite often, but I always enjoyed seeing it again. You entered their quarters via the guardroom, underneath which were the dungeons for prisoners. At the top of some spiral stone stairs was their sitting room, always rather dark, as the only light came through the original narrow slit window. Fortunately they had installed central heating or it would have been impossibly cold to live there in winter. After tea, the surgeon-cum-lawyer-cum-bishop said he would now like to conduct a little service in his chapel, and went off to change into appropriate robes.

He returned carrying a crook and wearing a mitre and what we assumed must be a Greek Orthodox bishop's vestments. Then the little congregation was shepherded down to the chapel where we sat down, and an incomprehensible and strange service was held. It was all in an unknown foreign language, which could have been modern Greek or ancient Greek or possibly just gibberish. We did not know when to stand or sit, or whether it was necessary at times to kneel. From his actions we deduced he was saying a series of prayers, and at one point when he stood up and addressed us in loud ringing tones, he must have been giving us a sermon. And all the time we could not understand a single word. I think the 'bishop' was hoping the ghostly Margaret Tudor would manifest herself to the fleshly one. But she did not oblige.

Another friendly neighbour was a retired general who lived in the only large house in Broad Oak. He was on all the local councils and committees and would help us with our problems whenever he could. We were always referred to by him collectively as, "Those two young ex-servicemen at Caldicott."

One day we were invited to a pre-Sunday lunch 'drinks party' at the general's house. This was a most unusual occurrence for us at that time. I dressed myself in one of my best Hong Kong dresses, stockings and light summer sandals. Harry put on a suit. We had not looked so respectable and tidy for a long time. But where was Guy? It was time we left.

Guy then appeared, very out of breath, having run uphill all the way from the bottom of the farm. "We've got to go down to Popland's Brake," he panted. "Amy (The Amiable Ayrshire) has had her calf down there in the middle of a great clump of brambles and won't let me go near her."

"Oh, damn Amy, and damn Popland's Brake," I muttered to myself and wondered once again who had been 'Popland' of the curious name. His brake was just the end bit of the vast Nant-y-Wain wood, which belonged to Cwm Madoc. Perhaps Popland was the man who had felled all the tall trees and then allowed the deforested land to cover its nakedness with scrub bushes and all kinds of nasty prickly things and bracken. And 'brake' was just another word for bracken, wasn't it?

So, clad in our glad rags, Harry and I followed Guy down the hill, and there in the centre of the thickest, prickliest blackberry bushes, stood Amy, head down, looking menacing and far from amiable. Entangled in the brambles behind her was her little, new-born calf. It took a long time to rescue the calf without getting impaled on Amy's lethal horns, but at length Guy was able to pick it up and carry the little creature uphill in his arms. Amy trotted along beside him alternately mooing lovingly at her child and bellowing angrily at us, until they were both safely ensconced in the empty cow maternity ward.

What was the time now? Good heavens, it was 1.30 p.m. and we had been invited for mid-day! Guy went to wash and dress, and I had to change my stockings which had dissolved into ladders.

"We'll go anyhow, even if we *are* late," Harry decided.

As we drove up the general's long drive, cars full of flushed-looking happy tipplers were driving erratically down it. But we carried on and spilling over with explanations and apologies, confronted our host and hostess.

"Never mind," they said kindly, "We quite understand. Come in and have a drink anyway."

Fifteen
Dogs, Cats and Rats

David Williams from Cwm Madoc, our kindly and courteous mentor, had said to Harry one day, "Mr. Tudor, I hope you don't mind me saying so, but I think you ought to have a cattle dog." He was always rather formal and punctiliously polite.

"Mr. Williams," Harry had replied in the same vein, "I am sure you are right. Where do you suggest I get one?"

"Well, Mr. Tudor, I just happen to have a litter of sheepdog pups, sired by my champion dog. There's one who's mainly white with a bit of black. That's the wrong way round: should be more black than white. You can have him cheap."

"May we come and see him, Mr. Williams?"

"Of course, Mr. Tudor, any time you like."

We went to see the pups and I wanted them all, but we came back with the 'mainly white' one, wrapped up in Harry's jacket. He already had a name - Roy - but to us he soon became known as Woggin.

"How do I train this pup, Mr. Williams?" Harry had asked.

"It's quite easy, Mr. Tudor. You just do everything you want him to do, and he'll copy you. And mind you take him with you everywhere."

That was why a small, white bundle was often to be seen asleep on Harry's cast-off pullover and why Harry could sometimes be observed galloping after the cows and barking at them. The puppy soon learned.

As Woggin grew older we discovered that speed 'sent' him. He loved accompanying the tractor when it was ploughing, and would tear along an adjacent furrow with his eyes shut tight in ecstasy. That was one of his problems. When we cut the ripe corn with the reaper and binder, a lot of rabbits always ran out of the last patch that remained standing. Village people would bring their dogs to the field and take home any

Roy as a puppy

Sonia with Roy when fully grown

rabbits the dogs caught. Woggin was always present and, seeing a rabbit emerge from the corn, he would set off in hot pursuit ... with his eyes shut. Sometimes he would run right past the escaping rabbit, and once crashed into a gatepost so hard that he concussed himself. Dear, silly, old dog.

On another occasion a litter of tiny coloured rabbits ran out of the corn.

"Stop! Stop! Don't let the dogs chase them!" I shouted.

We managed to catch the lot, five little brown, black and white and brown and white babies. Some tame rabbit must have escaped and mated with a wild one. I thought we could give these sweet little things to local children as pets.

It was a problem keeping them separate from the large company of cats we had acquired by then, so we popped the bunnies, for the time being, into an empty dirty-clothes bin. At bedtime it did not seem safe to leave them in the kitchen where some ingenious cat might discover how to remove the lid, so we took the bin and its contents upstairs to our bedroom. In the middle of the night we were woken by loud thumping noises. All five had managed to escape and were stamping around in the dark, as rabbits do when they are frightened. It was difficult to catch them with only the dim light that came from one torch and two candles, and involved much crawling around on the floor and under beds. But we recaptured the lot in the end and, after putting a very heavy weight on the lid, went back to sleep. The next day we found homes for them all.

It would be nice for Woggin to have a wife, we thought, and there was a suitable sheepdog bitch puppy at 'Evans the Moor.' She, naturally, was mainly black with a bit of white. I remember her first as a little round, black bundle with a fat tummy, and she too started her life with us with a fairly respectable name: Rumba. But in no time at all she had become Wigga-Wagga, or just Wigga for short.

When she grew up it was obvious that Woggin and Wigga were not compatible. For one thing Wigga did not treat Woggin with the respect due to an older dog. When he raced along furrows with his eyes shut, going all out, she would lollop effortlessly alongside, laughing at him in a rather superior, feminine way. So there were no Woggin/Wigga-Wagga puppies.

But Woggin's true love, whom he absolutely adored, was Nellie, Jack's 'almost-a-spaniel' dog. For four years at least, all Nellie's puppies, born and reared in the old, hollow oak tree, were fathered by Woggin. When she was in season he became dreadfully frustrated. Normally he slept in a large kennel outside the kitchen window, but when he was desperately in love we could not stand his nocturnal singing and howling. We tried shutting him up in the sitting room, but he was just as noisy there, and we were getting no rest.

At night, the incarcerated, love-lorn dogs were only about two hundred yards apart, as the crow flies. Woggin, in a melodious tenor, would sing:

"Oh Nellie, I love you, you're the only girl for me,
But the cads have locked me up, and I can't get free."

Nellie would reply in a frenzied coloratura-soprano:

"Oh Woggin, do escape! I am really at my prime,
We'd have such fun, if you'd come up and see me sometime."

The vet was told of our sleepless nights when he came to attend to a cow. "We're thinking of asking the doctor for some sleeping pills," we said.

"Don't do that," said the vet. "I'll give you some for the dog instead."

Woggin was given a crushed pill with his evening meal. Luckily he was not off his food, and in any case the proximity of numbers of determined cats made him eat everything quickly. He slept and we slept, although Nellie could still be heard singing a lonely solo.

It was because of the rats that we kept so many cats. We knew there were rats in the attics and in the granary, as well as in the separate farm buildings. The walls of the old house were about a foot thick and made of wattle and daub. I discovered this after reading a book about old buildings in Herefordshire, which also informed me that we were living in either an Ancient Monument or a Listed Building. Although not originally so, the walls had been made 'cavity-walled' by the activities of generations of rats.

The cellar which led down from the hall was to me a place of horror because of the stories narrated to us by village people. They were about the last, elderly, bachelor farmer who had lived alone at Caldicott before us. We were told he kept pigs in that cellar. This was his labour-saving idea, because there was a little stream down there, running through it from one side to the other. And, they said, sometimes pigs died in their dark prison, and he did not remove the corpses. After a lot of rain the stream ran faster, and someone had once seen a bloated, dead pig floating in the water. That was why, in spite of the resident barrels of beer and cider, I never went down into the cellar if I could avoid it. I might meet the ghost of a poor dead pig.

When we were upstairs we could hear the rats gambolling in the attics above, and each evening at 9 p.m. precisely, they descended to the cellar to have a drink. Nine o'clock was News time on the radio and as Big Ben chimed, some senior rat would say,

"Nine o'clock! Come on boys and girls, it's time for drinkies."

Then we would hear a scrabbling, squeaking noise in the hollow sitting room wall, as they scrambled down on their way to water. Five minutes later they would clamber back, more slowly. Once, greatly daring, we opened the cellar door just after 9 p.m. and shone a torch onto the floor. There they were, rows of grey bottoms and scaly tails; each head was down, lapping up water.

So cats were a MUST. I was pleased, for I have always loved cats, and there was no difficulty at all in getting a female kitten.

She was a nondescript little tabby, whom we called Tiger, but she had no personality. I was full of affection towards her but she did not reciprocate. I liked to cuddle her but she scratched back. With no parlour tricks at all, Tiger was definitely dull. Then our nice cleaning lady, who knew I liked tortoise-shells, gave me a tortoise-shell kitten. This one was at least attractive to look at, and had such a sophisticated and languid manner that we called her Tallulah, after the actress Tallulah Bankhead. In due course both Tiger and Tallulah had kittens, although we had no idea who their gentleman friend could be. All kittens, from now on, seemed to be born full of character. There was so much opposition that they had to vie with each other for our attention, and many of them developed individual party tricks to amuse us.

Harry added to the cat population by arriving in the kitchen one morning with two more: both coal-black female kittens.

"Here are Stinker and Smellie," he said. "I found them in a corner of the cattle-yard curled round a decomposing dead rabbit."

They smelt appalling. We guessed their mother was a Cwm Madoc cat who had had her kittens in the tunnels between the bales of hay and straw in the barn. Having decided they were now capable of looking after themselves, she had left a dead rabbit with them as iron rations and returned to Cwm Madoc. It was not easy to clean Stinker and Smellie as they were completely wild and fought back fiercely, snarling, spitting, scratching and biting. Wearing thick gardening gloves, I did my best with some warm water, soapflakes and pine disinfectant and eventually they became a little more fragrant. When they grew up they too met this mysterious and evasive tomcat, and each had a litter of kittens.

But, as Harry always said, "You can't have too much of a good thing." So, although we gave away many kittens, we always kept some. A lot of 'begetting' went on:

Tiger begat Tibby and Tibby begat Auntie B., and Auntie B. begat Tiny Toe Nails, and Tiny Toe Nails begat Tadpole, and Tadpole begat Charlie Boy and so on, *ad infinitum.*

And that was only one line of descent. Each kitten started life with a fairly sensible name, but this often degenerated into something ridiculous, like Tiny Toe Nails, for example.

I cannot remember all their names now, but I believe at one time we had about twenty cats. They were partially self-sufficient. I supplied them with bread and milk and if they wanted protein they had to go out and catch themselves some mice, rats or rabbits. We were gradually winning the war against the rats, and one day the Rat Catcher (or Rodent Officer as I think he was called officially) came to lay some bait in the house. He saw the large congregation of cats leaning hopefully against the front door. They had been ejected from the kitchen, as I could not cook with that gang sticking their experimental paws into my puddings and pies.

"Yes," said the Rat Catcher, "Every colour except green".

Our magnificent ginger and white male cat Cookapoo had originally been named Timothy, having been begotten by Tallulah, and it was his own fault that he was now called Cookapoo. He was a conversational cat and when anyone spoke to him he would reply, "Cookapoo." One day poor Cookapoo injured a front paw quite badly. On the vet's instructions he had to rest, with a bandaged paw, in a padded box by

Sonia and Harry with cats

the kitchen stove. Twice a day I changed his dressing and, being an intelligent and co-operative chap, he would hold the paw up to me. Soon he was also holding it up when he saw Harry. Harry would then raise his arm and say "Heil Hitler!" to Cookapoo.

After he had recovered, Cookapoo would salute us in this way whenever we met. One day Harry and a wartime friend were walking across a field when they noticed Cookapoo hunting along the bottom of the opposite hedge.

"See that cat?" Harry said to his friend, "He's a Nazi! I can make him do the Nazi salute."

"Bet you can't!" said the friend.

"Hello Cookapoo," shouted Harry, "Heil Hitler!"

Cookapoo looked up, raised his right paw in salute and went on his way.

Some of the cats set out quite deliberately to entertain us. One enjoyed tobogganing on his bottom down the corrugated iron roof of the woodshed and, if applauded, repeated this trick over and over again. Another, Auntie B., should have been an acrobat in a circus. If we ever felt a little bored in the evenings someone would say, "Do something, Auntie B." A wild, mad look would come into her eyes. Then she might leap up the curtains across the front door and hang upside-down from the top, suspended by just one claw. Or else jump onto the lower rungs of the legs of a chair and revolve at speed like a catherine wheel.

When it became her turn to beget, we were surprised to find one of her kittens had an extra toe on each paw, which made them look like bunches of bananas. This was Tiny Toe Nails, who, like her mother, was delightfully mad, and who gave birth later to Tadpole, who had a son called Charlie Boy. He looked and walked very like Charlie Chaplin, and all this line inherited the great bunches of toes.

"Them's lucky Herefordshire cats," they said in the village.

Our male cats had all been neutered, so who was the anonymous father of these non-stop offspring? He must be black and white, we deduced, as black and white kittens turned up in every litter. And then, one day, I saw him. I noticed Tiger, Tallulah, Susie, Stinker, Smellie, Auntie B., Tiny Toe Nails and all the other girls sitting round a wagon, gazing adoringly at something or somebody underneath it. There, smirking away, was the ugliest tomcat I had ever seen. He was covered with scars, parts of both ears were missing, he had only one eye and a broken tail. His general colour was black and white, but the patches of white on his face were most unsymmetrical and his beard lopsided. To crown it all he looked really evil and was obviously a cat of 'no fixed abode.'

It was not difficult to find a suitable name for him. We called him Creep. At that time the wartime radio show *I.T.M.A.* was still being broadcast, and in it was a character called Uriah Creep. His catchphrase was "Little do they know that I am hiding behind the settee" (or "in the cupboard" or "under the bed" or ...). It appeared our Creep was a well-known, vagrant, local character, but until now had had no name. Now people in Broad Oak started referring to him as "that ol' Creepers."

With him constantly around it was no wonder we were having this continuous cataclysm of kittens. He would have to go. Someone told us of a farmer about five miles away who was inundated with rats and needed cats. Creep was caught, tied up in a sack and driven to his new home.

There followed three or four Creepless days. Then I noticed the girls all sitting round that wagon again, and yes, Creep was back, crouched underneath, and wearing a victorious sneer.

Sixteen
To Market, to Market

As soon as we started farming at Caldicott it became very clear that we could not manage without a car. It was needed for trips to markets to buy small animals and for visits to local farm sales to buy second-hand farm implements.

Harry's sister Margaret offered to sell us her old pre-war Wolseley 'for a song'. A 'song' was all we could afford to pay, so we accepted gratefully.

At first we had no garage, so the elderly car had to live out in all weathers. It was rather frail already and this tough treatment did it no good. Then one day Harry and Guy solved the problem at a farm sale. I usually went with them on those occasions, because you never knew what treasures might be found there. The sales always started with the livestock, followed by the farm implements and then, as a finale, the bits of unwanted furniture and other odds and ends were sold. The small items were grouped together in 'lots', so if you saw a saucepan you fancied in one 'lot', you had to buy the bristle-less brush, coal shovel and six chipped enamel mugs as well. I bought my first primitive pressure cooker in this way. It was called a 'Pentecon', was made of vitreous enamel and had a screw-on lid which needed special cardboard washers to ensure a tight fit. The Pentecon was absolutely trustworthy. It never blew up in my face as subsequent more modern pressure cookers have done since. But that day I had not gone with them to the sale.

"What have you bought this time?" I asked when they returned.

"Oh, just a large hen house," they said.

It arrived the next day in sections. There seemed to be an enormous pile of dirty blackish separate pieces piled up in a great heap near the granary and a further stack of dirt-encrusted windows.

"How large is this house?" I asked Guy.

"About fifty feet by twelve feet," he said airily.

"That's as big as a bungalow! Where are we going to put it?"

"Harry and I have decided to use part of it as a garage, and the rest will make several hen houses."

They were right. Part was transformed into an adequate wooden garage, although any car we had from then on always smelt strongly of old hens. The rest became three poultry houses.

Hereford was our main market town. It was there that we usually went to buy small weaner pigs and very young bull calves. And later we returned there to sell those 'weaners' as 'baconers' and the calves as store cattle. The cattle market was very large and buyers from as far away as the U.S.A. and South America came to buy pedigree Hereford bulls. You could not miss the Texans, wearing high-crowned, broad-brimmed Stetson hats. They looked incongruous as they mixed with the English farmers who, when in their working clothes, often resembled their own scarecrows. But for market, some became positive dandies. The more prosperous ones wore well-cut breeches and highly-polished boots and gaiters. Their jackets were often of a rather loud check, as were their caps, and some adorned themselves further with fancy waistcoats. Farmers' wives were more drably dressed. Their husbands were the peacocks and they the peahens. The auctioneers were also snappy dressers and wore much the same attire as the well-to-do farmers, though usually topped by a racing-style trilby instead of a check cap.

None of these toffs came into direct contact with the animals. The cattle were prodded into the ring by lesser mortals, wielding long sticks and wearing gumboots and cotton overalls of a dun hue: a wise choice of colour. There was always a great deal of bellowing and shouting, parading and poking.

But it was not just a cattle market. Pigs, sheep, farm horses, poultry and other livestock were sold too, and on the perimeter were market stalls and the cheapjacks, who tempted farmers' wives with incredible bargains.

Their stalls were piled high with attractive-looking goods. One man sold crockery and, after he had enticed a large crowd around his pitch with his clever patter, would proceed to 'give away' his wares.

"Now then, ladies and gentlemen," he would shout in a penetrating voice, "You've all heard of Willow Pattern china, haven't you?"

"Yes!" the crowd would chorus.

"Well then, you know what a valuable investment it is? Right! I've got fifty sets here of genuine Willow Pattern dinner services. Take a good look at it, ladies. Go down the road to ....," and he named an expensive local shop, "and you'll have to fork out £30 for a set like this. But I'm not going to charge you £30. Oh no! I'm not going to ask you £20, or even £15, nor £10 neither. No! Tell you what I'm going to do! I'm going to *give* you these beautiful 24-piece sets for just a fiver! He hit his left hand palm with his right fist.

"Come along now. Who's the first lucky lady?"

A procession of lucky ladies would queue up to be parted from £5 and handed a large, heavy cardboard box. I was always very tempted; we were now eating off a 'harlequin' set of crockery with no two plates or cups and saucers the same pattern. But we would need all the space in the car for livestock.

Harry had recently cultivated a very fine, brushed-up handlebar moustache. It was a magnificent R.A.F. fighter pilot's operational model, which could even be seen from the back. When he first started buying calves and piglets in Hereford market the auctioneers did not know his name, and he was addressed as 'You-with-the-moustache', but soon, more respectfully, as 'Tudor, Caldicott' or 'Tudor, Broad Oak'. When we brought animals to the market to sell, the auctioneers would always ask, "Are you prepared to stand behind them, Mr. Tudor?" This was just their way of saying 'are you proud of them?' We always 'stood behind' our stock. I imagine that if you did not feel too pleased with your animals, you slunk away until it was all over.

Travelling in to Hereford Market was easy enough. But on the return journey we might have many additional passengers. Sometimes calves, sometimes piglets, sometimes both, and as we did not then have a car trailer, they had to travel on the back seat - in theory. However, the piglets and calves had other ideas and were always determined to sit in the front and drive.

Harry would say to me, "Get into the back with those piglets and/or calves and, for Heaven's sake, don't let them jump into the front and interfere with the driver." So I would sit in the middle of the back seat with piglets leaping all over me and an arm round each calf. They were impossible to control - I really needed to be an octopus - and one little pig always ended up sitting in the passenger seat, navigating.

Every so often we went to Abergavenny market instead. From Broad Oak we descended the hill into the old village of Skenfrith. After crossing the bridge over the river Monnow you were in Monmouthshire, which had Welsh licensing laws and, therefore, no pubs open on Sundays. That was why our Broad Oak Inn was so popular. There was a mediæval castle at Skenfrith and a water-powered mill where grain was stone-ground.

Abergavenny I had known well as a child. Guy and I had spent many school holidays there. This was because we holidayed alternately with our divorced parents. Our father had a rich friend who owned some salmon fishing on the River Usk and who often invited Daddy to join him. So while the rich friend stayed at the Angel Hotel in Abergavenny, Daddy took us to the less expensive and much more informal St. Ronan's Private Hotel. It was both more homely and more fun.

There were often three other children of our own age staying at St. Ronans, Binkie, Betty and Buster Miles. Their parents were salmon fishing enthusiasts too and, as well as the Miles family, we made friends with the slightly older Chadwick brothers, sons of the local big auctioneer.

On our first visit to Abergavenny market, I found the auctioneers were still called Chadwick and that the two sons, whom I had known so long ago, Peter and Reggie, had taken over the business from their father. They were just recognisable, and when I told them who I was, they said politely that they did remember me. I was told what had happened to the three Miles children and that Binkie, my special friend twenty years earlier, had been killed in the war.

However, we were not there for social chit-chat. Harry said he had noted four suitable calves, but they were being sold at the same time as some equally suitable piglets. So I would have to bid for the calves. I was to bid for numbers 3, 8, 11 and 18, and not go above a certain price. Feeling highly nervous, as I had never been entrusted with any bidding before, I stood close to the ring, the only woman amongst a gang of Welsh farmers. I reminded myself not to scratch my nose or ear, wink, or in fact move at all between bids. In the end I bought all four calves, but when the Chadwick brother auctioneering knocked them down to me, he could not remember my married name and I was too frightened to open my mouth. So the four calves were bought by some saintly woman, apparently called 'St. Ronans'.

The only other market we visited was Gloucester, which was said to be particularly good for pigs. It was about thirty miles from Broad Oak and I remember the first expedition to market there well, because of the uncooperative behaviour of the Wolseley. The car was rapidly falling apart and in its death throes. The sunshine roof would no longer stay shut, so unless I held on to it all the time, we travelled exposed to the elements in every kind of weather. The horn had packed in too, and

Harry had bought a rude-sounding bicycle horn. If we were ever going fast enough to pass anything Harry would tell me to lean out of the window and hoot my horn. This had a devastating effect on dear old ladies wobbling along on bicycles. That horn brought out the worst in Harry and made him behave like Mr. Toad.

And now the radiator had started boiling over when the car climbed hills. So as well as the horn, we also had to carry bottles of water. On that day we were towing a trailer full of pigs and there were many hills on the road to Gloucester. As the car came to the boil on every incline, we had to stop constantly to let it cool down and to refill the radiator. It was taking a very long time to get to Gloucester that day and we were afraid we might miss the pig market altogether. Many of the people we had previously hooted at now passed us, glaring balefully as they recognised the car.

So we decided there and then to buy a slightly less decrepit and more reliable second-hand car, and soon our local, friendly garage owner found us a younger car, a Vauxhall, in much better condition. We had noticed that there was an open-air second-hand car market at Hereford where 'old bangers' were sold by auction. We took the Wolseley there - it just about made it - and waited to see it sold, or not sold. We did not feel we could 'stand behind' it, so we hid in the crowd. To our surprise the auctioneer seemed to be getting several bids, and eventually it was knocked down to someone for £95. £95! We had expected to get £40 or £50 if we were lucky. £95 would go some way towards paying for the Vauxhall. "Wasn't that good!" said Harry, "I never dreamt it was worth as much as that."

When the car sale was over we went to the auctioneers' office and asked for the money for the Wolseley they had just sold, less commission, of course.

"Sorry, I didn't sell it," the salesman said. "Didn't get one bid."

"What! We saw you taking several bids,"

"Oh, those weren't proper bids," he replied, "They were just imaginary ones."

We had to drive the ancient vehicle slowly and carefully home, and I cannot now remember its eventual fate.

Harry with one of the pigs

Seventeen
The Great Pig Hunt

All Caldicott Farm pigs seemed cheerful and contented. Mothers and babies were allowed to wander about in the paddock in front of the house and the others could range around in the orchard.

Howie Dainty Boy came out for exercise too and on hot summer days greatly enjoyed wallowing in the muddy pond on which the house agent had suggested I kept ducks. One could almost hear him grunting, "Mud, mud, glorious mud ..." He would enter the pond as a Large White boar and emerge as a large, black boar, completely coated in rich-smelling sludge.

Pigs are affectionate, sociable and intelligent animals; talkative too if you can understand their short, low grunts. But it was the baby pigs that I enjoyed most. When they were loosed out into the paddock, even staid, old Mum would cavort about in an undignified and abandoned way, while her progeny would gambol around her on short, stiff, little legs, snorting, squealing and playing games of tig.

Quite often a piglet was born who needed intensive care. He was usually the runt or 'little Harry' of the litter. Sows often seemed to be equipped with ten or twelve teats, and sometimes, inconveniently, gave birth to eleven or thirteen piglets. It was like a game of musical chairs: the last arrival could find no entry to the milk bar. Then the little Harry or Harriet would come to live in the kitchen for a while, till he or she was fighting fit. Like Cookapoo, the invalid slept in a warm box by the stove and was fed at regular intervals from a baby's bottle. Bundled up in an old piece of blanket or towel, it did look very like a human baby as it sucked away noisily. I can quite understand how the Duchess's baby in *Alice in Wonderland* turned into a piglet. When wrapped in a shawl the only difference between the two is that a human baby does not have quite such a large, pink snout.

It was on a day after we had returned from market that we had the Great Pig Hunt. We had filled the car trailer in Hereford with small weaner pigs and then, when we got home, poured them straight out of the trailer into an empty pig hut with a surrounding run. Well satisfied with our morning's work, we went off to have some food.

Returning later to check on the piglets, we found the house and run empty and a hole in the chain link fencing. There was no sign of stray piglets in the orchard, but the ground was soft and Sherlock Harry noticed a trail of little, sharp pigs' trotters heading towards the gate. "They've gone that-away," he deduced. Noses down, we tracked them into the lane, past the garage, along a muddy cart-track and into the top of the Watercress Field.

From there we spotted them for the first time, right down at the bottom end, about to squeeze under the gate into the field where Krupa had made his wonderful haycocks. "View-halloo!" we shouted and galloped after them. We made good time going downhill but when we turned the corner at the bottom, there was not a piglet to be seen.

"I bet they've gone into Popland's Brake," I said.

The cows who were grazing in the field thought so too. They were all staring with interest at that prickly place: mostly brambles, briars and blackthorn. Every bush there had thorns and it was excellent cover for small pigs. Then we caught sight of the tips of two little corkscrew tails in the undergrowth. "Tally-ho!" we yelled as we pounded across the grass.

It was not easy to winkle the piglets out of their hiding place. They knew we could not flush them from the depths of the bushes, and stood huddled together staring at us defiantly from underneath their white eyelashes. There was a short pause while we all panted in unison. Suddenly they were off again, through the briars, brambles and thorns, and hurtling straight up the hill, in the direction, thank goodness, of the house and buildings.

They had the advantage of us. We were standing knee-deep in a forest of thorns and were already bleeding profusely. Their agile, little bodies could charge through the small, open spaces at the bottom of the undergrowth. But we had to fight off every thorny branch in our path. It took us much longer to emerge from the copse, and we were tired now and short of breath. Our clothes were ripped and our arms and legs lacerated.

One field from home, with the piglets winning the race by a distance, we spied Fizz outside Poppy's stable. "Fizz!" we both cried, or at least tried to cry, but with no breath left after running some distance uphill, we had been rendered speechless and not a sound came out of either of our mouths. So we prayed silently instead that Fizz might see us, or the piglets, and we waved our arms at her in desperation, pointing to the door of Poppy's stable.

Suddenly Fizz noticed the procession of little, grunting pigs racing towards her and in the distance, the two demented figures waving their arms about and pointing. The penny dropped. She opened the stable door. The piglets streamed in and Fizz slammed it shut. We collapsed where we stood, with lungs heaving and legs like jelly. When we could once again move and speak, we staggered up the rest of the hill. The lesson we learned that day was: 'Always examine the fence carefully before putting small pigs in a run.'

While rubbing soothing ointment into my sore arms and legs later that day, I had a great thought: "Harry," I said, "I've just realised that everything that cut, pricked or scratched us in Popland's Brake this afternoon was a 'b' thing."

"They certainly were b..... things."

"No, not the kind of 'b' you mean. I was thinking of brambles, briars and blackthorn. Even splintery bracken stalks."

"B..... things in every sense," Harry reiterated with feeling.

There was always one particular pig whose acquaintance I deliberately did not cultivate. This was the pig destined to be turned into pork, ham, bacon and so on, for our own consumption. I believe we were officially allowed to kill one pig every year for this purpose. If we did we had to surrender all the bacon coupons in our ration books. Many other people, farmers and cottagers alike, also reared one pig, and when it had been slaughtered and cut up into its numerous component parts, gave portions of it to friends. You might be lucky and get a joint of pork, or if not, some liver or sausages. They say you can eat every part of a pig except its squeak. Though how about 'bubble and squeak?'

So as well as the higher-class pieces for bacon, ham and pork, there were also sausages, liver, heart, kidneys, trotters, tongue, brawn and mysterious, supposedly edible bits, called chitterlings. These pallid parts of a pig's anatomy looked depressing and unpromising to me. When I discovered what they really were - the pig's intestines - I vowed never to buy them. They were officially 'offal' and our butcher who usually had very little to sell would get quite excited when he had some. He would whisper, conspiratorially, "I've got some lovely chitterlings today!"

The weekly ration of meat for which we had to hand over coupons from our ration books was very small. In spite of this our butcher wielded great power. This was because offal was not rationed. He could, and did, reserve it for his favourite customers. So even if his counter appeared quite bare, there was always a chance of something exciting concealed beneath it. This might only be produced if you were the sole customer in the shop. It paid to smile and exert any charm and sex appeal you had on this elderly man, clad in a blood-besplattered, blue-and-white striped apron and battered boater hat.

"Thank you very much Mr. Probert," I would simper, as I handed over the coupons for four small chops. "Have you, by any chance, got anything off the ration - a sausage or two, perhaps?"

The shop seemed quite empty, nothing hanging from the hooks on the ceiling, only dummy packets of stuffing on the shelves and the old, traditional sawdust on the floor.

"Yes", he would leer, "Just for you my dear, three nice hearts."

After first glancing to right and left through the shop window, he would bend down and swiftly wrap something in newspaper. I would thank him profusely and leave quickly before another registered customer could arrive and note I had two parcels from the butcher in my basket instead of one.

Our local amateur pig slaughterer and butcher was Mr. Thomas the Post Office, although his only connection with the Post Office was through Mrs. Thomas, who was the Broad Oak postmistress. When the day came for the annual ritual sacrificial ceremony, I stayed inside the house and played the radio at full volume. I was a coward and did not want to hear the pig's dying squeals.

Then it was our turn to distribute pieces of pig to as many people as possible. I was left with the remainder, including the hams and the reproachful-looking head, which always made me think of John the Baptist. This had to be made into brawn. Mr. Thomas had taken away the two sides of bacon to cure. Later he returned them and they hung from hooks in the larder. Unfortunately the bacon always tasted rather 'reasty' to me. This must be a local country word as I cannot find it in any dictionary. It means strong and over-salty.

Eighteen
Broad Oak

Broad Oak was not really large enough to be called a village. It was just a hamlet clustering around the old Broad Oak Inn. In its heyday the village had undoubtedly been quite important. It lay on one of the roads crossing from England into Wales and at the Broad Oak Inn stagecoaches had stopped and horses had been changed. Quite possibly passengers had stayed in the inn overnight. Now all that was left to denote its former status was the one-time toll house, occupied by Jack and Flossie, the stunted remains of the famous Broad Oak itself and the inn.

The gloomy interior of the pub was not helped by large areas of brown paintwork and the dark, wooden wainscots, tables, settles and benches. The wood gave off that curious smell - half sour, half sweet - that used to be found in old pubs. It was the smell of timber which had been slowly pickling in beer and cider for centuries. Nowadays that distinctive aroma has been sanitised out of existence. There was always a good fire burning in both the saloon and public bars, and in the big back room where farmers had their meetings and occasional dinners.

We had a Post Office too in Broad Oak, presided over by Mrs. Thomas the Post. Her little white cottage housed the Post Office in her front room, and she was our nearest neighbour, just three or four minutes walk from the farm. Mrs. Thomas, with her pale face and white hair pinned into a bun, sold stamps and postal orders and dealt with the mail. She also dispensed information about anything going on in Broad Oak, although she was not one to gossip. I very much valued her wise counsel. When I had a problem and there seemed to be no suitable person around to advise me, I would walk up to the Post Office and confide in Mrs. Thomas. She was soothing and practical, full of motherly guidance and reassurance. One of her two daughters was a nurse at the local hospital and was often at home when off duty. So I often took my gashes and cuts to be inspected by this expert, who would often tell me they needed to be stitched.

"Is Mary home?" I would ask.

"What have you done now, dear?"

"I've sliced my hand with the bill-hook again."

"Oh, you should keep away from that nasty thing."

"Yes, I know I should, but the trouble is I enjoy using it."

Mary would come through from the back room and inspect the wound and usually say, "Yes, that needs a couple of stitches. Better see the doctor. In the meantime I'll put a nice tight bandage on for you."

The only other amenity in Broad Oak was the Mission Church. The mother church was in St. Weonards and I suspected that the vicar there considered the inhabitants of Broad Oak completely heathen and beyond redemption. Why else would there be only one service every four or five weeks, on the first Sunday of the month? Most of the village people went to chapel in Garway, which also had the nearest shop. The churchgoers of Broad Oak were few in number, but included a local schoolmistress, who played the organ. Harry and I thought it was our duty to make an appearance on this one, important Sunday every month, but we did not realise we would be obliged to sing. The schoolmistress played the organ well and raised her voice in song. No-one else did. They stood for the hymns and read their hymn books, but kept their mouths shut. Neither of us could sing, although we much admired the voices of Anne Ziegler and Webster Booth, who we frequently heard on the radio singing duets from musical comedy and operetta. However we felt compelled to join the schoolmistress and added our tuneless duet to her solo. I'm sure nobody enjoyed our wailing but we did at least try.

Since there were no buses passing through Broad Oak, any trip I took alone to Ross had to be by bicycle. These were always shopping trips, and the six-mile outward ride was enjoyable since it was partly downhill and partly on the flat. At this point all my shopping bags were empty. The return journey was different. Always over-optimistic about how much I could carry home, I would first stuff a full bag into the shopping basket in front. Then the outsize saddlebag would be filled. That left at least two or three more bags to be transported. One would ride on my back and the other two dangled each side of the handlebars. Unless they were evenly balanced I would find myself veering dangerously to the right or left, and I always had to dismount and push my load up the last mile of hill.

A few cottages lined the road to Garway and my much-treasured Mrs. Owen lived in one of them. She came to do the rough one morning a week, and did her best to deal with the build-up of deep litter underfoot in the farmhouse. I could not offer her any aids to housework, but she made do with old-fashioned brushes, brooms, a dustpan and brush and an inefficient wooden Ewbank carpet sweeper. This swept quite well, but as soon as it had collected a certain amount of rubbish and dust, was immediately sick and regurgitated its meal all over the floor. Mrs. Owen found it better to fling old tea-leaves over the floor and carpets, and then sweep them up again after they had attached themselves to the dirt, chaff, hay, straw and worse. A few hours after her weekly whip-round, the house looked just as bad.

She, it was, who suggested I saw a Mrs. Roberts when I complained about some unsightly warts which had suddenly appeared on my hand.

"You'd better go and see Mrs. Roberts: she'll charm them away in no time."

"How can she do that, Mrs. Owen?"

"Well, she's a white witch, see!"

"A white witch! I don't think I like the sound of that!"

"Oh, no dear, she's quite 'armless. Mrs. Roberts can set bones and make medicines out of 'erbs. Girls go to see her about their love affairs, you know, and she always knows when there's a storm coming."

She told me where this gifted woman lived, and I took my warts to her. I found her living in a roadside cottage inside a garden filled with different herbs. Tall drifts of comfrey were growing in the background and I could recognise the everyday mint, sage, thyme, rosemary and marjoram, but there were many others I did not know.

There were no signs of either a broomstick or a black cat. Mrs. Owen had told me that the prefix 'white' cancelled out the frightening connotations of the word 'witch' and that many people came to consult Mrs. Roberts rather than make the long journey to the nearest doctor. I tapped on her door and a lady, massive in both height and girth, asked me in. I had been told she was double-jointed, although she wore so many layers of skirts and aprons that I would not have noticed if she had had two wooden legs. White witches were often double-jointed, they said, and I remembered a double-jointed girl I had been to school with, who could contort her body into the most surprising shapes. I wondered if she had been an incipient witch.

Mrs. Roberts scrutinised the disfiguring warts on my hand and then handed me six small, earthy potatoes.

"Go 'ome and bury them in your garden, m'dear, and by the time the new moon 'as come, they'll be gone."

Unable to see any connection between my warts and her potatoes, I thanked her and did what she said. A few weeks later my hand was wartless.

The white witch was not Broad Oak's only association with the supernatural; there was also the Holy Thorn.

Once again, it was Mrs. Owen who told me about this miraculous annual happening. I had heard of the Glastonbury Thorn and knew the legend connected with it: how Joseph of Arimathea is said to have planted his staff, made from a piece of the Holy Cross, at Glastonbury, and how the thorn bush that grew from his staff flowers every Christmas. The Broad Oak Holy Thorn, in a field near the village, was said to have grown from a twig picked from the Glastonbury Thorn, and it too flowered at Christmas. Groups of people went to witness this inexplicable winter flowering every year, and I was invited to go with them. How I wish I had gone, but looking back I realise I must always have been too sleepy and too tired to stay awake after midnight. That was the hour they set off on their expedition. But one year someone brought me back a sprig from the thorn: real hawthorn blossom in full bloom in the depths of winter.

In my mind the Holy Thorn was also connected with another Christmas legend: country people told me that at midnight on Christmas Eve all the domestic animals that are shut up for the night in stables, such as cows, horses and donkeys, kneel in memory of the Holy Babe. Every year, during our farming days, I always intended to stay awake and go into the stables and cowsheds to see if this lovely story was really true. But, alas, sleep always overcame me.

Now, so many years later, I regret missing my chances to witness the two annual miracles. One, at least, I know really happens.

Nineteen
Bread, Butter and Cheese

Guy's prophecy of self-sufficiency was beginning to come true. But how about the bread, butter and cheese he had included in his prediction? Their manufacture was a complete mystery to me and I guessed they might prove difficult.

"I'd like to try to make some bread," I told a friend.

"Have you tried the 'Grant loaf'?" she asked.

"No, what is it?"

"My dear, it's absolutely out of this world, and so easy to make. I'll lend you the book, then you can try for yourself."

The book was called *Your Daily Bread* and had been written by a Mrs. Doris Grant. In it she told her readers how nutritionally worthless white bread was, after all the healthful parts had been extracted from it, whereas whole grain, stone ground, wheat flour, which had had nothing removed, was amazingly good for the system. What is more, it was almost a universal cure for most day-to-day ills, being chock-a-block with vitamins. It included 'B', which gave you energy and drive, 'E' which helped to alleviate stress and prevent heart attacks, and bran which promoted 'regularity'. This sounded just what the doctor ordered, but the thought of what I imagined would be a time-consuming job put me off. And all that kneading and proving and rising and waiting. Would it be worth the energy expended? Time and energy were both in short supply in those days.

Still, imbued with a beginner's enthusiasm, I tried the undeniably simple recipe for the Grant loaf. This method of bread-making involved the minimum of work and time, and no kneading at all. To my surprise, after first producing a batch of chapatis, and then a collection of brown bricks, I suddenly got the hang of it. I found myself making beautiful, brown loaves that tasted so good they scarcely needed the addition of butter or jam. The bread problem had been easily solved.

Now for the butter. We took as much milk as we wanted from the nurse cows. There was nothing remotely hygienic or T.T. (Tuberculin Tested) about it. Either Fizz or Harry milked straight into a bucket. Then it came into the dairy, uncooled, and was poured into large, flat, metal pans and left until the cream had risen to the surface. This was then skimmed off and put into a separate container.

It took me many hours of hard work before I discovered how to turn our hand-skimmed cream into butter. The ration was still some minute amount like two ounces per head per week. A traditional wooden butter churn was out of the question; we would never have enough cream. But advertised in the invaluable *Farmers Weekly* were little portable glass churns, which held, perhaps, between three and five pints of cream. We bought one. I poured in the collected cream, screwed on the lid and started to turn the handle, to which small wooden paddles were attached. After fifteen minutes nothing had happened, although my right arm ached. I decided to ignore the churn and read a good book while the cream was being agitated, stopping to peer at it every now and then. It still looked exactly the same: no sign of butter. Perhaps the cream was too fresh? I would leave it for a day and then try again. No butter materialised on the following day either, but I was very much enjoying the book, even if my churning arm sometimes felt as if it was dislocated from its socket.

Maybe I should have bought *The Complete Dairy Maid* and been perusing that instead of a thick book called *Forever Amber*. This was a juicy Restoration romance: the heroine, Amber, was forever having torrid affairs with everybody who was anybody in the Restoration period, culminating, inevitably, with King Charles II himself.

And then one day, quite by accident, I stumbled on the secret of how to make butter in a small churn. I had been diverted from my task for some reason, and the cream had been waiting for a time near the cooker and had become a little warm. When I at last started to rotate the handle again, and simultaneously devour another thrilling chapter of *Forever Amber*, I heard an unusual splashing noise coming from the churn. I looked, and there they were, lumps of real butter, floating around in lots of watery looking buttermilk. I had cracked the code, and from now on butter making was no longer a difficulty. But with no further prolonged churning sessions, I took a long time to finish that book.

Now I had to fulfil the last of Guy's prophecies, and learn how to make cheese. This was not going to be easy either, with our limited amount of milk and cream. 'Cottage cheese' happened very often when milk went sour, and I economically strained it through butter muslin. We all thought the resulting lumpy mess boring and much too bland. We wanted a cheese with some bite to it. Surely there must be some quick, easy, labour-saving way to make it?

I did not have *The Complete Dairy Maid* or any similar modern book, and had no intention of becoming a complete dairy maid either. There were far too many other daily duties to perform. When I told my friend Susan about my intention, she lent me a very old book, published in the nineteenth century, which she had found in a second-hand bookshop. It had been written by an anonymous 'lady', for the use of other 'ladies', who had been brought up in a town, but who now found themselves forced to live in the country. From the contents it sounded as if they must all be married to country squires. The book, in the form of a series of letters, covered everything from the care of canaries and cut flowers, the making of cider and crumpets, the culture of crops and cuttings, the keeping of cows and cures for poultry diseases, to the teaching of cookery and clothes-making to cottagers.

It also included sixteen closely printed pages on cheese-making. After reading her meticulous instructions on how to make Gloucester, Stilton, Cheshire, Cheddar, Wiltshire and even Parmesan cheese, I decided the procedures were far too complicated and prolonged for me. Some of them went on for months.

So I studied the back pages of the *Farmers Weekly* once more. It actually had some simple cheese recipes suitable for a busy farmer's wife, and I found instructions for making a soft cheese rather like Caerphilly. It may even have been a kind of Caerphilly.

The ingredients were simple: whole milk, rennet and salt. The equipment needed was simple too: just shallow, circular, metal moulds that sat on finely woven straw mats. The milk, after it had been curdled by rennet, was placed in the moulds, and whey gradually drained out through the mats, leaving eventually a softish, quite palatable sort of cream cheese. This could be eaten ten days later and we rather liked it. It made a pleasant change from the rationed mouse-trap Cheddar.

These newly acquired simple skills made me feel quite smug. Perhaps one day I could pass an 'O' level in Farmwifery?

Twenty
How We Nearly Didn't Go to the Ball

The day of the Hunt Ball dawned bright and clear, as they used to say in nineteenth-century novels. It started for us with a shopping expedition to Ross-on-Wye in our new, green car. Actually it was the same car - the second-hand, black Vauxhall - but we had had it resprayed jade green.

The reason for such an extravagant action was this: at that time, about five years after the end of the war, most cars, even new ones, were black. This had almost caused an embarrassing incident one day in Hereford market. Having finished our business there, we jumped into the car and drove smartly home. But not very smartly: the car did not seem to be pulling as well as usual. Glancing around, we noticed an unfamiliar hat and coat on the back seat, and some shopping we did not remember doing. I got out and examined the number plate. Yes, this car was definitely one of the same litter, but it was obviously not ours. It did not have any straw and manure stuck beneath the mudguards for one thing. Nor was the back seat sprouting stuffing, or littered with more straw and a goodly amount of mud. We drove back to the market car park and re-parked the car exactly where we had found it.

There did not seem to be a hue and cry going on, and our own car, with the well-known dirty raincoats inside, was where we had left it, two rows away. We crept in and drove away again, rather more smartly this time.

It was then we decided to have our Vauxhall sprayed a distinctive colour: something that would stand out amongst all that sombre black. There cannot have been much choice, otherwise I do not think we would have chosen the vulgar shade of jade green. But in for a penny in for a pound, we thought. So: "Shall we have the Vauxhall's flutes done a different colour?" Harry suggested.

"Yes! Let's have them painted red, and the wheel hubs red too," I added, altogether carried away. "And we might as well have the trailer sprayed to match the car."

The '*tout ensemble*' certainly looked both different and distinctive. The Vauxhall was now very easy to spot in any car park and as we drove through villages people cheered and waved. They probably thought we were advance publicity for a travelling circus.

After we had done our shopping in Ross that day, we decided to treat ourselves to lunch at one of the hotels. At the end of the meal I noticed that Harry was looking worried and was searching first the table, then his lap and finally the floor by his feet.

"What have you lost?" I asked.

"My teeth," he whispered. He had two false teeth on a small dental plate.

He caught the waiter's eye: "Have you found any ... er ... teeth on the plates you've taken back to the kitchen?"

The elderly and venerable waiter looked slightly shocked. He could not believe his ears. "What did you say you had lost, sir?"

"Two teeth," Harry lisped. He was doing his best to speak without opening his mouth more than a centimetre.

"I'll go and look sir," said the waiter.

"Sorry sir," he said on his return. "No teeth have been reported found in the kitchen."

Harry then went and searched the gents but with no luck. "I can remember sneezing hard as we walked along the street on our way here," he said, "perhaps I sneezed them out. We'd better walk back the way we came, and I'll look on the pavement, if you'll look in the gutter."

There were no signs of teeth or crushed denture in either place.

"Well, I can only think I must have swallowed them," Harry declared.

By then I was beginning to get a little worried, as I knew the plate had two small hooks on it. So we did the sensible thing and went to our doctor, who conveniently lived in Ross.

The desk, chairs, curtains, carpet and bottom half of the wall in the doctor's surgery were all shades of brown. The rest was either dark green or cream. It was not a cheerful place. In one corner was an old weighing machine with little, round weights for stones and a sliding metal bit that indicated the pounds. On the wall behind his desk was the eyesight chart with the letter 'F' glaring down on all his patients, and in a corner was a tall, wooden cabinet with many drawers of all sizes. Various surgical instruments lived here, including the strong pincers he used occasionally for the emergency extraction of teeth. In one drawer I knew he kept a supply of sharp needles and threads for sewing up wounds. He had often sewn up small parts of my anatomy.

Compared with today he seemed a most versatile man, prepared to pull out teeth, lance boils and perform most minor surgery. Leading off the surgery was a pharmacy where he mixed his four or five basic cures for most simple troubles. Patients began to feel better almost immediately when they had been given a bottle by the doctor. The 'cures' must have been as much due to faith as anything else.

"What seems to be the trouble this time?" enquired the doctor, giving us both an appraising look. He was used to seeing the Tudors - we were both accident-prone - and he could not decide which of us was the patient.

"I think I've swallowed my teeth," said Harry.

"What! All of them?"

"No, just the two I have on a plate ... the plate has two little, metal hooks on it."

"Dear, oh dear," sighed the doctor, "I'm afraid you'll have to go to the cottage hospital and be X-rayed. Here's a note."

At the cottage hospital Harry was told to remove all his clothes, which were then confiscated by the matron. Wearing nothing but a hospital gown and covered with a blanket, he was wheeled on a trolley to the passage outside the X-ray room and abandoned there. I visited him several times from my seat in the waiting room, but he appeared to have been forgotten. I enquired when my husband could expect to be X-rayed, but was fobbed off with talk of the X-ray department being very busy that afternoon. As far as we could see, no-one had either gone in or come out of the room for a long time. Neither could we hear any voices or sounds of activity from inside.

After two or three hours had passed, Harry was at last wheeled in and X-rayed. The hospital doctor studied the plates and reported no sign of teeth or denture anywhere in Harry's interior. He admitted he too had been a bit concerned about those two hooks.

"Go home and get on with your usual activities," he said, "but if you should suddenly feel severe pain, come back here immediately."

So we were able to go to the Hunt Ball that evening after all. Hunt Ball! Yes, it was most unusual for us in those days to gallivant like that. The local Master of Foxhounds of a small hunt was also a farmer, a very nice man with an equally pleasant wife. They had become friends of ours and we had been invited to join their party, to begin with for dinner, and afterwards at the Hunt Ball. I was to wear an evening dress for the first time since we had returned from Hong Kong, and Harry would wear his white tie and tails. I had not yet seen him arrayed in all his glory.

At first Harry was conscious of his slightly bizarre, gap-toothed appearance when speaking or smiling and was unnaturally silent and solemn. But as the evening wore on and he took in more alcohol he threw discretion to the wind and relaxed, talking, smiling and laughing with abandon. But I could not relax. I watched him nervously. Although he was minus two eye-teeth and did not have fangs, he still bore a curious resemblance to Count Dracula. I was waiting for the moment when he would suddenly go pale and clutch his stomach as either the teeth bit, or the hooks got entangled in some part of his digestive organs.

But nothing like this happened. Harry cavorted happily into the small hours. We never did discover what happened to those teeth.

Haycocks at Caldicott
Watercolour by Lady Eva Tudor ('Chinkie')

Twenty-one
Don't Put Your Turkey On The Train,
Mrs. Worthington

Becoming day by day more enthusiastically self-sufficient, one of us remarked, "Wouldn't it be nice to rear our own Christmas turkeys? Then we could give home-grown turkeys to all our friends and relations as Christmas presents. Solve that problem!"

The Poultry World was keen that year on the Broad Breasted Bronze breed. For me this immediately conjured up a vision of a body of well-built, warlike Amazon women. We added another 'How To' book, on turkey rearing this time, to our rapidly expanding reference library.

It seemed to be quite plain sailing at first. We bought several sittings of turkey eggs and tucked them under a series of broody hens. These particular hens were lucky, as they did not have to endure the usual 'cold turkey' treatment meted out to broody hens. The method used to cure them of their maternal instinct consisted of prison for a few days in a raised coop with a draughty, slatted floor, and no nice hay or straw to sit on. This was another useful lesson I had learnt from my father.

Four weeks later each of the favoured hens found she was mother to six fluffy grey and gold speckled chicks, and when the time came for mothers and chicks to be parted I consulted the turkey book again.

Oh calamity! It said, "Turkey chicks, or poults, as they are now called, must not be allowed to set foot on the ground until they are almost full-grown. This is because of the danger of picking up 'blackhead', a disease peculiar to poultry and primarily to turkeys. All poultry must be reared on wire mesh floors in enclosed, raised runs."

It was sad for the hitherto free-range baby turkeys and made another job for Harry and Jack, who had to set to and build a very large run, totally enclosed in wire netting and balanced on wooden legs. This was connected to a roomy hen-house, also raised from the ground. It looked rather like an Indonesian stilt-house.

Then the two dozen turkey poults were placed in their elevated home and from now on could only survey the world through wire mesh. We did our best to cheer and placate them with large bunches of sow thistle, which turkeys love. Luckily the still uncultivated kitchen garden, which now contained the turkey house and run, was full of sow thistle, so we were able to do, simultaneously, a little almost painless weeding.

Like the other poultry sections the turkeys had to be shut up at night. We found the ideal time for this was about 8.15 p.m. Usually at this hour Harry and I were glued to the radio listening to *I.T.M.A.*, *Ray's a Laugh* or *Much-Binding-in-the-Marsh*. But there was always an interval about halfway through the programme, when the comedians stopped being funny for a few minutes. The announcer would say, "And now for a song: the delightful Miss Clara Cluck will sing *I'm Just a Girl Who Can't Say No*, from *Oklahoma*."

This was our cue. One of us - we took it in turns - would dash out of the sitting room, through the hall, kitchen and scullery, across the back yard into the kitchen garden, up the path, take first turn on left and arrive panting at the turkey house. Then shut the pophole and return swiftly by the same route. We would return to the sitting room in time to hear the soprano declaring in a cracked voice for the final time, "I cain't say no!" as we would collapse into an armchair.

When the turkeys had successfully come through the trauma of their adolescence, they were allowed to come down from their wire floor and walk around freely on the ground again. But before we released them we were anxious to know which were 'stags' and which were 'hens'. The male turkey for some confusing reason is called a stag. The hens would be more succulent to eat, so we hoped many of the young poults would be female. We also planned to keep one stag and six hens as breeding stock for the following year. At this stage in their lives they all looked identical: uniformly grey with undeveloped wattles.

Fortunately Harry had perfected a useful party trick: how to imitate a mature stag turkey. It involved him in bending down, dragging his arms along the ground, hissing and finally exclaiming, "Haa-arm-de-bobble-de-gobble." This cry caused all the young, potential stag turkeys to become very excited, and they would start strutting up and down in the cage, showing off in front of the young hens. After this they would puff up all their feathers and open their wings, dragging the tips along the ground. While they did this they hissed, and their heads and incipient wattles would change colour to first dark pink, then crimson and lastly purple. By then, feeling very emotional, their faces would have turned turquoise blue in colour. Meanwhile a lump of skin above their eyes grew longer and longer, until it hung down over their beaks. Their tails would fan out and then they too would declare, "Haa-arm-de-bobble-de-gobble."

On one rare occasion when we had some rather sticky visitors and had become desperate about how to entertain them, we asked:

"Would you like to see Harry sexing the turkeys?"

"Oh, yes please," they replied, very intrigued. The ensuing show kept them spellbound.

Once released from their high-rise prison the turkeys were free to wander wherever they liked. But because of the many predatory foxes they had to be locked up at night. They preferred to sleep out, and usually chose to huddle together in a huge clump of stinging nettles.

"You dunderheads!" I said to them. "You complete clots! Hasn't anyone told you about foxes?"

Woggin was very good at driving them out of the nettles and back into their house. But they retaliated by starting to roost in the lower branches of big trees, and we gave up. After all, foxes cannot usually climb.

As Christmas approached most of the turkeys were killed and we had a great plucking and cleaning session in the scullery. All this was organised by Flossie, who brought her team of versatile girls. Wearing sacking aprons, we sat in the scullery, which for this important occasion was lit by a Tilley lamp and heated by a tall, circular Valor stove.

My memory flew back to dark, nocturnal cypher duties in an R.A.F. trailer in Italy during the war. Just such an oil heater had been my only companion from midnight till 8 a.m., and I had toasted my lone processed cheese sandwich on its patterned top.

Flossie instructed us what to do and, while we worked, she kept us entertained with news of the latest scandals in the Broad Oak district. We plucked away diligently at the turkeys, and feathers and fluff flew everywhere, including into our hair and eyes and up our noses. This caused a great deal of sneezing. When the plucking was over there was also the unpleasant, smelly business of drawing the entrails. All this was known as 'dressing' the turkeys, although to my inexperienced eye it seemed more like 'undressing' them.

Then lastly, with the aid of many skewers, they were forced to assume their correctly compact, buxom shape.

Some of them were labelled and sent by train - so reliable in those days - to various friends and relatives. We heard that they had all arrived safely, but one of our more candid relatives, in her thank-you letter, remarked: "Unfortunately the turkey on arrival was too high to eat." We really did not want to know this, and hoped the other recipients' Christmas presents arrived in a better state. We vowed not to give the same seasonal gift to anyone the following year.

Twenty-Two
The Broad Oak Show

The high spot of the village year was the annual Broad Oak Show. It seemed strange for such a little place to have its very own show, but we found it was actually a collective show for several neighbouring villages. Kind David Williams always lent his top field alongside the road for the event, and on a Friday evening in July the main marquee and the large tents were erected.

There were several of these. The first and most important was the bar tent, followed by the stewards' tent: a meeting place for important persons wearing rosettes in their lapels. The marquee was given over to the exhibitors and their competing classes. Fruit, vegetables, flowers, jams, cakes, wines and eggs etc., were all eligible. Next door stood the controversial tent in which the baby show was held: sounds of bawling babies and the indignant voices of offended mothers emanated from this one. And lastly there was the refreshment tent, dispensing cups of tea, buns, sausage rolls, pies and sandwiches. Outside a brass band played Souza marches and Strauss waltzes loudly and enthusiastically, and there were sports for the children. Later in the afternoon there would be pony races, with genuine bookies in attendance.

On this very special day the local ladies arrived arrayed in their best clothes: colourful floral frocks and flower-trimmed hats to match. They made their rather derogatory remarks about their rivals' cakes, jams and wines in loud whispers as they walked slowly round the exhibitors' tent, evaluating every item on show.

"Can't think why she's got First for her fruit cake. It sags in the middle, doesn't it Gladys?"

"Yes, Megan. Just like a saucer it is."

"That jam of Olwen's hasn't even set, and they've given her Second. Your jam is much better, Gwynneth. Unfair I call it."

"Lovely brown eggs Mrs. Tudor's got. Wonder how she does it? Dyes them in black coffee, I expect!"

I usually entered the classes for best sponge cake, best jar of jam and best plate of six brown eggs, but with no luck - not even a 'commended' - until I got the Marans. They were a breed of French hens who were incapable of laying any eggs except large, beautiful, dark brown ones, the colour of a horse-chestnut. I had read about this Gallic breed in *The Poultry World* and was bowled over by the description of the hens and their eggs. I sent for a sitting.

All the eggs hatched and in due course I knew I had six cockerels and six pullets. The most handsome cockerel was kept, the five others sold, and the small French contingent were given a little house near the granary.

Though but girls yet, they already had a matronly look, like middle-class French ladies of 'a certain age'. Maybe it was the general effect of their well-groomed, black-and-white feathers and the jaunty, crimson hat they each wore. They kept themselves to themselves, and murmured softly to each other in French. I imagine they could not talk English 'hen' like the Light Sussex tribe or American 'hen' like the Rhode Island Red tribe, or even broken English like the Italian immigrant Leghorns. The Maran eggs were works of art. I never sold those. They were kept for home consumption and were so perfect in colour and form that I did not really like cracking the shells.

I talked to them quietly and politely in bad French: "*Est-ce-que vous avez des oeufs pour moi ce matin?*"

"*Oui, Madame. Nous avons déjà cinq oeufs,*" they would reply.

So with my French hens laying five or six reddish-brown eggs for me daily, I was confident of winning First in the brown egg class. Unless someone else had discovered my secret and bought some Maran hens too.

That year I was alone. Harry had had a brief look around and gone home. Studying my programme I saw that after the childrens' sports there was to be a 'ladies' race' for the first time. Quite a novelty and good for a laugh ... it would be rather fun to enter, I thought. After all, a decade or two earlier, I had been called 'a good little sprinter', and surely with all the energetic farm work and constant running up and down hill, I must be fit? No-one was there to advise me and say, "Don't be ridiculous," so I paid my entrance fee and walked up to the start. So did several other girls and women, younger than me. But when we got there we saw the opposition, in the form of an athletic-looking lady wearing running gear and spiked shoes. She was having her legs massaged by her trainer.

"Oh, *she's* here!" someone whispered, "goes round all the shows, she does, and wins all the races. We don't stand a chance."

I was wearing a 'play-suit', a pre-war outfit of top and shorts with a matching skirt to don if you needed to feel more respectably clad. I took off the skirt. And I could not run in sandals with heels, so I removed them too and handed them to an acquaintance. This was a very stupid move. David Williams had mown a swathe of grass for the race track, but there were a lot of thistles among the cut grass. When the race started I found I was pounding through a carpet of thistles. I could either stop running and retire, or persist, spurred on by the pain. The athletic girl in the spiked shoes won, of course, and I was not even placed, though not quite last. Never mind, I would go now and see what the judges had thought of my cake, jam and eggs. They had thought nothing at all of the first two, but the eggs had a blue card lying in front of them saying, 'First Prize'. I had won five shillings! So even if I were no longer fleet of foot and was an indifferent jam maker and a mediocre cake baker, I was at least a good egg. I collected my prize money wondering how I should spend this windfall, and hobbled home. It was hard to decide which foot to limp on.

"How on earth have you managed to get so many thorns in the soles of your feet?" Harry asked, as he went to work with a sharp needle and tweezers later that evening.

The Williams' second son, Gordon, had become a great friend of ours. I felt a little sorry for him because he knew his elder brother would inherit Cwm Madoc and his only chance of becoming independent would be to rent a farm, which was not easy. Gordon loved talking. It must have been difficult to get a word in edgeways at home, with ten or twelve people sitting down to every meal. So he started to come over most Sundays to join us at a late breakfast and to exercise his voice and views on life. All the feeding of animals would be done first and then I would cook an unusually enormous breakfast: orange juice, cornflakes and porridge, eggs, bacon, sausages, fried bread, mushrooms and tomatoes in season, followed by toast, butter, jam, honey and marmalade, all washed down by tea or coffee. That was the menu. With both so much to eat and to say, the meal lasted from 11 a.m. to 1 p.m. Then Gordon would mutter something about going home for his dinner, although where he would put that, I could not think. Harry would always walk with him as far as the boundary between the two farms. If during the afternoon I needed Harry, I knew where I would find him. He would be leaning against one side of the boundary stile, with Gordon leaning against the other side - both still talking.

Gordon took a great interest in my poultry ventures, and was very keen that I should have some geese. I was equally determined not to have them.

"Why don't you like geese?" Gordon asked, exasperated by my refusals.

"Well, I don't like them for two reasons. Firstly, I detest the mess they make of the grass, marching about on their great flat feet, you know perfectly well what I mean, Gordon; and secondly, I'm afraid of ganders."

I told him about the fierce gander who used to charge us when Harry and I rode our bicycles across his field. This was towards the end of the war when we were just married and allowed to 'live out' from our R.A.F. station.

But Gordon was persistent and one day presented me with three 'gull's' eggs. It was a *'fait accompli'*; I could not be impolite and insist he took them back. Apparently goslings were called gulls in that part of Herefordshire. In due course the eggs hatched out into three quite attractive, fluffy, long-necked little creatures. It was when they were old enough to roam around without their foster-mother that they ran into trouble. Serious, sad trouble, involving Woggin. It was not his fault: he was just trying to do someone a good turn.

Woggin despised all our cats, except for one, the little black cat called Smellie. While he occupied the whole hearth rug and forced all cats to sit behind him, Smellie was allowed to lie between his paws and enjoy the best of the fire. When she had kittens, Woggin noticed her gradually moving them, stage by stage, nearer to the house, and he started carrying Smellie's kittens for her, holding them carefully by the scruff of their necks, as she did. So when one day he met three, still fluffy-necked goslings wandering round the farm by themselves, he decided they must be straying kittens: yellow ones. Each was picked up in turn by the neck and deposited carefully by the garden gate. But this mode of transport had been too much for the little gulls, and they now lay in a row, lifeless, all with broken necks. I found three small corpses lying side by side and Woggin gazing at them with a bright 'haven't I been a clever dog' look in his eye. Thus ended my only attempt to keep geese.

Twenty-Three
Have You Any Wool?

So far we had steered clear of keeping sheep. But there were a lot of sheep next door at Cwm Madoc who did their best to break into our fields, where they considered the grass was greener. The mass break-ins often happened on moonlit summer nights. We would be woken by a clamour of baa-ing and maa-ing as the jubilant sheep jumped one by one through the gap they had just made in the boundary hedge.

After quickly flinging on a few clothes, we would collect the two dogs and hurry down to the scene of the invasion. Then we would all do our best to drive the sheep back through the hole they had created. For some reason they were never able to find it again, and would panic in loud, despairing bleats:

"De-ar, oh de-ar!"

"Wh-ere's the ga-ap?"

"We ca-an't find the ga-ap!"

"It's somewhere ne-ar he-re,"

"But wh-ere? Whe-ere?"

"De-ar, oh de-ar."

"It's he-re, he-re, he-re!"

"We've just fou-nd the ga-ap!"

When - hot, tired and angry - we did finally get them all back onto Cwm Madoc land, we would mend the hole as best we could, cursing the sheep and wondering whey they could not sleep at night like other more sensible animals.

It was Gordon's idea that we should share a flock of sheep with him. He was very keen to have some sheep of his own, but there was not room for them on his father's heavily stocked farm. So a small flock of forty breeding ewes was acquired, and it was agreed that if we supplied the grazing, Gordon would supply the know-how.

The scheme worked well, but I was horrified at all the attention sheep had to receive, as well as the quite revolting diseases, parasites and pests they could be attacked by; as many and as varied as the Plagues of Egypt. The sheep itself seemed a badly designed animal, unable to get back onto its legs again unaided if it was lying on its back. To me it looked too bulky for its little, spindly lower limbs, as if the body and head had been created first, and the four inadequate legs screwed in as an afterthought. Little lambs are sweet, but adult sheep, if not actually mentally deficient, give the impression of being a bit simple.

Still, with Gordon in charge of this aspect of stock-keeping, all went well. He and Harry, who was under instruction, worked together and I merely observed. Perhaps if I had been given a chance to get to know the sheep better, my view of them would have been less jaundiced.

Harry had been using the then comparatively new system of electric fencing for a few years with great success. It was employed to control the grazing of the beef cattle on kale and new leys of grass and clover, and was powered by electric batteries.

Now he and Gordon thought they would try this technique for penning the sheep, instead of using hurdles. But we soon learned that sheep are not as easily trained as cattle. First a long, narrow rectangle of grass near the road at the top of the orchard was fenced off. This was to be the training ground. It was entirely surrounded by electric fencing wire, including a wire across the gateway which led into the farm lane. This wire could be removed to let the sheep in and out of the electrified enclosure.

Then one day, after the now-customary, gargantuan Sunday breakfast, Harry and Gordon drove the forty ewes up the farm lane and through the gateway into the now enclosed piece of orchard. They then rejoined the connecting wire across the gateway and switched on the electric current.

As with all grazing animals entering a new pasture, they spread out to inspect the boundaries. In no time at all the wires were on the ground, the fence posts had been knocked down and there were sheep all over the orchard. "The battery must have run out!" we exclaimed. Then with Woggin's help the sheep were rounded up and driven back onto the enclosed grazing strip. When the electric fence had been re-erected and tested, the electric shock was found to be as strong as ever. We could not understand why the sheep seemed to be impervious to it. I can still remember the technique we used for testing an electric fence without giving ourselves a nasty shock. Wearing gumboots or rubber-soled shoes, we would pick a long, thick blade of grass and hold the tip against the wire. If the fence was working correctly we would receive a mild shock. It was not advisable to test the fence without taking these precautions.

Just as we were about to give up in despair, the sun was blotted out by an immense black cloud, a wind sprang up from the west and suddenly we were standing in drenching rain. The sheep, with their heads lowered against the wind and rain, moved swiftly to the shelter of the roadside hedge. But then, one after the other, they jumped back in confusion as their wet fleeces touched the live wire. "So-ome na-asty wa-asp ha-as stu-ung us!" they bleated. A few turned back to the other side of the fenced rectangle, but as soon as they reached the far wire they received another shock. There were loud, complaining cries of, "It's not fa-air! We've been stu-ung aga-ain!"

The rain stopped after a while, but now we knew the answer to the problem with the electric fence. It was quite simple: water. A hose-pipe was run across from the buildings, and both the ground under the wire and the sheeps' coats were kept wet with occasional waterings. After two days they had learnt to respect the wire, but had eaten all the grass. The sheep would now have to be moved. Another area further down the farm was wired off, the connecting wire across the gateway out of the orchard removed, and the sheep driven towards it.

But the ewes had learnt their lesson: "O-oh no-o! We-'re no-ot go-oing thro-ough the-re!" they wailed, piling up one against the other in front of the gate. Nothing would induce them to cross that invisible line: they had been stung there before.

So there was nothing else for it. One by one, Harry and Gordon picked them up and carried them over the imaginary wire, until all forty were safely in the farm lane and on their way to the new pasture. We had learnt a lesson too: that the wire must terminate at posts on either side of the gateway. The sheep soon came to know that this area was free from unpleasant stings. The original electric fenced rectangle was kept as a training ground.

Twenty-Four
Haymaking and Harvesting

When haymaking and harvesting time arrived we always found we were short of workers. It happened every summer. All the other farms around us were busy for the same reason, so we had to look farther afield for temporary help.

One year the son of a friend came to help us out. Simon, now at university, was an agreeable young man, strong and willing to try anything. The only drawback was his hay fever, but we did not know about that until he had settled in and started to sneeze and sniff and mop his streaming eyes. Never mind, we had advertised for a further strong, young man who was just about to arrive. On paper this one sounded ideal. "My name is Robert," he had written. "I am very large and intend to become even larger." We wondered what he meant by this. He went on to mention that he was a failed medical student. His luggage, when he arrived, contained a pair of chest expanders, which explained his cryptic remark.

By an unhappy coincidence, however, Robert also suffered from hay fever. So those two workers were virtually useless during the haymaking season, although they did their best. Poor Robert was not only allergic to pollen but also to thistles. He had not got the horny hands of a genuine son of the soil, more the delicate, soft, white ones of a potential physician. His fingers swelled up whenever they were attacked by thistles, which happened daily. The poor fellow spent long evenings in the kitchen, applying poultices to his fingers and painfully removing prickles and thorns. He punctuated these activities by ringing up a series of female relatives in Scotland and telling them sad stories of his farming experiences, always starting with the words "Oh Aantie, it's awful!" We could hear him: he had a loud voice.

Scenes from Caldicott farm with retouching by Lady Eva Tudor ('Chinkie')

Still, Robert stuck it out bravely, and each Saturday went into Hereford to do some shopping. His purchases were always the same. Each week he returned with yet another pair of beautiful and expensive brown brogue shoes. They were lined up, all bright and shining, on the floor in his bedroom, and he spent much time when not poulticing, polishing.

For some while I had been plotting to have my friend Tommy to stay at the same time as Harry's friend Dick. Not for any romantic match-making reason - Dick was already married - but simply for the pleasure of being able to say I was doing something or other with Tom, Dick and Harry.

Tommy was an ex-W.A.A.F officer friend from the war, and when I had enticed her to visit us, I found her a very practical help as she was a country girl by birth. Tom used to lend a hand cutting and bunching watercress in what I always thought of as '*my* field'.

At the house end of the rough lane that led to this field, Harry had positioned a bird-scarer, aimed at deterring gangster pigeons or rooks. This was because one year the young seedlings of some crop had been completely destroyed by marauding birds. The scarer was set to go off with an ear-shattering bang every three minutes. It certainly scared me, and I would leap high in the air if within fifty yards of the explosion. So I would try to time my journeys down the lane for immediately after a bang. My strategy did not always work: the bird scarer was erratic and sometimes there would be two reports in quick succession. It was extremely nerve-wracking.

For some unrecognised and still not understood reason, I had mentally taken possession of this little fragment of the farm. It was not my field at all, being just a useful piece of permanent pasture, suitable for grazing bullocks. But to me it was an enchanted place, and I felt strongly protective towards it. We called it the Watercress Field. Many years later when I saw my first Alpine meadow in full summer flower, it reminded me of that field in Herefordshire.

The Watercress Field was of irregular shape with a spinney of trees and bushes in the middle. Through this ran a narrow, deeply set brook. Round the edges of the spinney lay an unusually luxuriant carpet of wild flowers: primroses, cowslips, oxlips, violets, bluebells and wood anemones. There may have been others. Growing in the pasture itself was a variety of meadow flowers including early purple and spotted orchids. And that was not the end of the magic. In the surrounding hedges there were spindle bushes festooned with coral and orange fruits in autumn and several hawthorns each supporting a load of mistletoe, for this was mistletoe country.

At the top of my field was a round, clear pond fed by a spring. This was where the watercress grew. We ate a lot of this as it was free, and all the iron that it contained must have helped to keep us so healthy. I used to wade around in the water, cutting large handfuls of cress, which were then made up into rubber-banded bundles. Feeling a little like one of the street sellers of old London, although not knowing an appropriate song or cry, I would take my basketful into Ross. A small greengrocer there was glad to give me thrupence a bunch and sell it five minutes later for sixpence.

But my little paradise was always under threat. The War Ag. still paid two pounds an acre for ploughed-up permanent pasture. Both Harry and Guy looked at the Watercress Field with a farmer's eye and were blind to its botanical beauty. Each year I had to do a ritual grovel and plead for it to be spared from the plough. It was always given a reprieve, although a cattle shelter was built at the top one year, and after that store cattle grazed there every winter on the 'foggage', or old dried grass.

I would retreat to this place when I occasionally felt a little depressed, and search for more wild flowers to add to my long list, or wade about in the clear, cold water of the pond. Cutting watercress was soothing and therapeutic. Though not realising it at the time, I suppose, I was beginning to become a conservationist.

174

Twenty-Five
A Great Decision

Four years had passed in which we had learnt a lot, much by making expensive mistakes. We were very happy at Caldicott and even beginning to be successful in a small way.

Farms were graded A, B or C by the omnipotent War Ag. and when we had taken over Caldicott it had been a run-down grade C farm. Now, after much hard-slogging, it had been up-graded to A. We even had 'farm walks' round our land occasionally, when other more 'proper' farmers progressed through the fields and buildings, observing what was being done by these newcomers.

But contented though we were in our new farming life, we realised we could not make much more headway, unless we went in for milk production. This would give us the financial security of a monthly milk cheque. Selling milk commercially at Caldicott was not possible because of the lack of mains electricity needed to work a labour-saving milking machine, and as it would also be impossible to produce T.T. milk in a fourteenth-century cowhouse, we would have to build a modern milking parlour too. There was no doubt about it: the lack of electricity was holding us back.

The absence of electric power also increased my work considerably. The chore I hated most, and which had to be done daily, was filling the many oil lamps with paraffin, trimming the wicks and worst of all, cleaning the glass lamp chimneys. These seemed excessively fragile, and were very easily broken, either when the flame was rashly turned up too high or when I was carefully washing the black paraffin smoke off them. In fact they kept "coming to pieces in me 'ands." I detested the smell of paraffin too.

The many people who came to rough it with us at 'Cold Comfort Farm' insisted that they positively *enjoyed* going to bed carrying either a lighted candle or a smoking oil lamp. Both of these were kind to the face, but hard on the eyes.

On one hot summer's night there was a terrific thunderstorm which crashed and flashed away noisily, directly overhead. It retreated for a while and then returned, retreated once again and then gave us a second repeat performance. It was impossible to sleep and, in any case, I always used to worry about the cows during summer thunderstorms. There they were, out in the fields, without protection of any kind. They could easily get struck by lightning.

So we lit our little lamps and decided to settle for a night's reading instead of sleeping. A wide, natural shelf, about four feet high, ran around the walls of the room and I had put surplus books on it. We each grabbed a book at random.

"What have you got?" I asked Harry.

"Mine's rather appropriate," he said. "It's called *Casting Out Fear!* What about you?"

"Oh, I've got *Five Years Hell In A Country Parish* by the Vicar of Rusper. I remember this book: it's rather good."

I marvelled once again at my parents' strange taste in reading matter.

The second most-hated domestic chore was ironing. The first deep, long drawer of the kitchen dresser was always stuffed to overflowing with clean, but creased, laundry. No electric iron meant I was forced to use primitive flat irons heated on the top of the Crag cooker. The irons' hot handles had to be wrapped in a duster or something similar and, as a concession to our more delicate pieces of laundry, the flat sole of the hot iron was clipped into a kind of removable metal shield.

I loathed using this old-fashioned method because it was so time-consuming, and that was why we bought a patent iron heated by paraffin. This had to be pumped regularly like a Primus stove or a Tilley lamp. But the hot, hissing contraption frightened me and I was always afraid it would blow up in my face. The Primus stove exploded regularly and much of the time I had neither eyebrows nor eyelashes.

Nasty things usually happen in threes. Our third 'nasty' was a paraffin cooking stove. We had bought this at a farm sale for a bargain price. Unlovely in appearance, it stood on a metal stand and had four burners and a flimsy metal oven that could sit over two of them. It was said to be 'in good working order' and the idea was that it would only be used in an emergency: for instance on occasions when the Insulted Crag was having a particularly spiteful fit of the sulks, and was either loathe to burn, or had gone out altogether.

There was no room for the paraffin cooker in the kitchen. This was just as well. It would not have fitted in at all with the rustic decor. But there was plenty of space in the scullery, so we planted it there with its back to the wall. The cooker was supposed to burn with a clean, blue flame: if it did, it was working correctly. Before long I discovered that it too could behave like a prima donna. Often when a cooking emergency arose I would get nice blue flames burning, shove a saucepan or two on top, or even sometimes the oven, and leave it while I tried to cajole the Insulted Crag into working again. Then someone would open the back door and create a slight draught. This was all it needed to go completely berserk. The blue flames would immediately change to a dirty yellow, and produce foul, greasy, black soot. I would return to find the scullery full of smoke, the saucepans blackened and, if I were baking, bread or cake covered with black, oily icing.

No, paraffin and I were not compatible. So it seemed electricity would solve many problems, both large and small.

Rather sadly we made the decision to sell the farm and start again somewhere already equipped with mains electricity, where we could have a milking herd *and* electric light, electric irons and other nice labour-saving items once again.

Now more farmers with appraising eyes came to walk round the farm, but for another reason, and their wives came with them, to inspect the farmhouse.

This had been improved a little, since we now did at least have indoor sanitation, hot and cold water, and a bathroom. I had spent many happy hours inside the house slapping distemper on the walls and paint on the woodwork. My memory insists that my decorating always took place while listening to Test match commentaries on the portable radio. But I suspect I must also have listened to other less memorable programmes while 'doing-it-myself'. Emulsion paint had not then arrived in the shops so I had to use flaky distemper applied over an initial sealing coat of size. I chose cream distemper for all the walls. It went well with the beams and traditional solid oak floors.

Some wives walked round silently with noses a-twitch and made no comments. I hoped they could not smell the last, lingering traces of the most recent rat to die under the floorboards in the sitting room. I hardly dared show them the interiors of wall cupboards, larder and dairy, as the distemper flaked away in those places like dandruff, almost as soon as it was applied. Damp, I suppose. Other wives were kinder and said they thought the olde-world look was rather attractive.

The reaction I remember best was that of a middle-European gentleman, who, I guessed, had probably been a refugee in the last war. He had no wife at heel, so he inspected the house as well as the rest of the farm. Then he gave us his considered opinion:

"Your land - I like," he said. "Your 'ouse - I like, but your coo-'ouses, I do not like."

It was sad that he did not appreciate the beauty of the authentic fourteenth-century byres.

We could not help noticing that one youngish man, who lived nearby, had probably been hooked. He returned again and again to have yet another look. As he had a French wife and six children they would be able to make good use of the five bedrooms. We were not surprised when, in the end, he was the one who bought our farm. He also agreed to buy Rumba, alias Wigga-Wagga, as he would need a good cattle or sheep dog, and promised to take over any working cats for whom we could not find homes. Although he did not know it immediately, he was also taking over Creep, lurking, invisible as usual, under a farm wagon.

Then we arranged for Roy, alias Woggin, to go to live temporarily with some friends in the north of England until we had found another farm.

Watercolour of Caldicott Farm as seen from the orchard, by Lady Eva Tudor ('Chinkie')

Twenty-Six
Sale This Day

Now it was our turn to have a farm sale. Everything was to be sold, except the furniture which would go into store in Hereford until we found our new farm, wherever that might be. I am still not sure whether our sale could be described as 'lock, stock and barrel'. 'Lock' we had already sold, 'stock' was still to be sold, but what did 'barrel' mean?

There was much to be arranged. First, a suitable early autumn date with the auctioneers in Hereford. This had to be advertised widely in the local press, with a condensed list of everything to be sold. There would also be a printed catalogue.

Farm sales usually started with the livestock, and horses were sold first. But we were not selling Poppy. She was now at least thirty-five years old, and we could not bear the idea of her being taken away, frightened, to travel to a cruel death.

Poppy had loved the cows. After so many years in their company she must have forgotten she was a horse and considered herself one of them; but a superior cow with a wicked sense of humour, and she enjoyed playing tricks on them. One of her favourite pranks was to wait until they were all plodding patiently through a gate *en route* for milking. Then she would charge from a distance, creating great havoc and consternation in the narrow gateway, and scattering them in all directions.

Whilst we had been waiting to move into the farm, we used to bicycle over every day to check on Poppy and the cows. It was cold and wintry weather then, and the three of us would sit on a gate like a row of crows to eat our sandwiches. There was little filling available for the sandwiches at the time, and one day they contained just thin, insipid slices of luncheon meat. To pep them up I had added lots of mustard. While we sat and munched, I felt warm breath on the back of my neck and was nuzzled by a soft velvet nose. It was Poppy expecting a tasty morsel - an apple perhaps, or at least a core.

"Go away Poppy, dear. You won't like sandwiches and we haven't got an apple today," I told her. But she butted us each continually in the back and tried to stick her face between our shoulders to snatch something.

"Oh, all right!" said Harry. "Try this," and he handed her a mustard sandwich.

Poppy took a bite and then we heard a horrified snort. We looked round in time to see her expressing complete disgust. With her head in the air, she turned her upper lip completely inside out, revealing all her old, brown-stained teeth.

Hearing that we were selling up, an unpleasant individual came to offer us quite a lot of money for Poppy. He did not want her as a working horse, but as horse-meat. He was surprised that we did not accept his generous offer. No, we told him, the horse was not for sale. She had been a good and always willing friend to us and, whatever had happened before, we knew the last five years of her life had been happy. We arranged for our kind and understanding vet to come and dispatch her with a humane killer, instantly and painlessly.

So the livestock would consist of the cows, calves and store cattle, pigs and assorted poultry.

The poultry were a big item in the sale. Apart from the various flocks of laying hens, there were now several thriving throngs of young cockerels, just ready for the table. This enterprise had been continuing for some years, though not always so successfully.

Initially I had contacted poultry dealers from the East End of London, who advertised for young cockerels in the farming and poultry periodicals. The dealers were a cunning spiv-like bunch, who wore shabby double-breasted suits and scuffed patent leather shoes. They arrived driving tall, top-heavy vans crammed with empty poultry crates, and haggled with me about my beautiful, plump, ready-to-eat cockerels. When they saw them they sneered, picked them up, assessed their weight and sneered again. "Not fat enough," they said disparagingly. "Not enough breast meat. Can't give you more than such-and-such per pound for these."

"Nonsense," I would retort. I had expected fifty percent more, but the dealers always won. There were further batches of half-grown birds off stage, ready to occupy the cockerels' houses. Obviously the dealers wanted a more Mae West type of bird. Something like our Broad Breasted Bronze turkeys.

The Poultry World again provided the answer to the problem. They showed photographs of Indian game cockerels. These stocky, rather belligerent-looking, short-legged birds were certainly broad-breasted. They reminded me of fat Japanese wrestlers. They even had a similar menacing pre-fight stance. *The Poultry World* said that if these cockerels were crossed with Light Sussex hens, the resulting progeny would have the same bow-window shape as the game cockerel with the Light Sussex's white plumage. We bought several Indian game cockerels and left them to run with Light Sussex hens. Then the eggs were incubated and both the pullet and cockerel chicks were sold at four months for the table. I never had any trouble selling these double-breasted birds for a good price.

After the 'live' stock had been sold it would be the turn of the 'dead' stock. This comprised the farm machinery and all the implements, including the old horse-drawn ones we had discovered hidden in the vegetation. At the very end of the sale the odd bits of household equipment and furniture we now no longer needed would go under the hammer. I was delighted to be able to include, in this category, all the oil lamps, the terrifying paraffin-powered iron and the flat irons. The unreliable and malevolent paraffin cooker was to be resold, once again vouched for as being in 'working order' (provided you never opened a door while it was alight). If we had been psychic we would have held on to all those oil lamps. They and the flat irons were destined to become valuable collectors' pieces less than twenty years on.

We were so busy putting our house and farm in order that there was little time to feel sad. But I did miss cheerful little Wigga, when she went to live with her new owners for a while before returning later to the farm with them.

Early on the morning of the sale, as instructed by the auctioneers, we made a 'ring' in the orchard out of bales of straw. All the animals to be sold that day were to be paraded there before being auctioned. We prayed for a fine, dry day and that a big crowd of potential buyers would arrive. A field was set aside for the implements and another as a car park. Even earlier, the auctioneers had stuck a 'Sale This Day' notice on the gate, and 'To the Sale' signs had been placed at strategic points at surrounding crossroads.

Soon after 9 a.m. a mobile canteen selling cups of tea, sausage rolls and sandwiches arrived. It was a good sign that they considered our sale worth attending. Groups of people started to arrive and mooched about gazing at the machinery and poking it with their sticks. They found their way to the places where the animals were penned and poked them too. When they became bored with this they wandered round the outside of the house and peered through the windows. I glowered back and drew all the downstairs curtains.

A farm sale was a social occasion, often spent drinking, and meeting and talking to friends. There were some who went just for a day out, without intending to buy anything. They contrived to look casual and uninterested, masking their natural curiosity and nosiness. It was all part of the fun.

But to offset these drones, good friends might also come to keep the bidding going and run up the prices. This, of course, was encouraged by the auctioneer. We hoped some genuinely keen buyers were among the crowd, and that if dealers came they would not conspire to form a 'dealers' ring'.

Then the auctioneer from Hereford arrived, wearing a yellow waistcoat for the occasion. He and his clerk positioned themselves on top of some straw bales, and we were off.

He started selling the livestock, all of which had numbered labels stuck on their behinds. Each cow in turn was fetched from the cowhouse and paraded, attached to a halter, round the ring. Most of them behaved well, although one highly-strung lady called Jezebel took fright when she found herself the centre of attention. The auctioneer's chanting and the rows of staring faces were too much for her and, with a desperate look in her protruding eyes, she jerked her head in the air, pulling the halter out of Jack's hand. In a split second she had picked an unguarded spot in the ring and jumped over the bales to freedom. She was quickly caught but, after this exhibition of her unreliable temperament, no-one was very keen to buy her and she was sold for a song.

Then it was the bullocks' turn, followed by the calves. They were prodded and persuaded into the ring, loose, but the gentle Hereford crosses were not bothered by the crowd and the auctioneer's shouts.

Next in the catalogue came the pigs. The sows were fetched and ambled around amiably, followed by the porkers and weaners, and lastly, Howie Dainty Boy 15th himself appeared. He was looking particularly well-fed and healthy. This was not at all surprising, as he had recently had an extra ration of protein. The cat Stinker had chosen to have her most recent litter in his pen. "How sweet!" we had said at first as we watched the great, fat boar gently nuzzling the little kittens. But he was only waiting for them to grow a bit larger. "How disgusting!" we said when we discovered later that he had eaten them.

The poultry were the last of the livestock to be auctioned. They had all been incarcerated in poultry crates. We could hear them cursing and swearing and see rows of indignant heads protruding between the slats. Some had automatically laid eggs on the wooden floors and were now angrily stamping on them. They made good money and so did the unusually broad-breasted Indian game cross table birds. "Well done, boys and girls. I am proud of you," I told them. While the animals were being sold I had wandered around in the background, anonymously I hoped, experiencing in turn sadness, disappointment, pleasure and annoyance. I did not feel so sentimental about the machinery. The price mattered, of course, but I had not become attached in the same way to the tractors, implements and wagons. Yes, Creep was observed sitting under one of those.

But after the auctioneer had dealt with the farm equipment, I watched with interest the disposal of the household chattels. I felt sorry for the unfortunate woman who inherited the vindictive paraffin cooking stove. I heard her being assured by the auctioneer, previously primed by me, that it was 'in good working order'. He exaggerated: I had omitted the word 'good'. But would anyone want to buy the smoky oil lamps and the flat irons? To my surprise a rather well-dressed man, definitely a townee, bought them all ... for a pittance.

"Who was that?" I asked a friend.

"Oh he keeps a big antique shop in Hereford," she replied. He must also have been clairvoyant.

The sale was over now. Hauliers and farmers with trucks and vans were loading up the livestock and machinery. Our two tractors were driven away and, after the pig houses, hen houses and arks had been removed one by one, the orchard looked empty and desolate. All that was left to remind us of the day was a round, churned-up, muddy piece of grass and an unusually large number of cowpats.

The evening felt so still, so quiet. I missed the familiar, happy sounds of grunting pigs, clucking hens, crowing cockerels and the gentle mooing of cows. Tonight there would be no feeding or milking. Tomorrow the dairyman would arrive with pasteurised milk … in a bottle.

The merry-go-round had stopped. We felt dizzy after the ride, but now, at last, we could dismount.

Twenty-Seven
Packing Up

Now all we had to do was to clean and tidy up all over the farm, especially in the farm buildings and the house. Everything must be left spick-and-span for the new owners.

During those five years we seemed to have accumulated a mountain of rubbish. Had we never thrown anything away? No, apparently not. I could remember us both saying so often, "That might come in useful some day," and stuffing whatever it was into either the attic or a store shed. We were both, in our different ways, squirrels by nature. The squirrels' hoards were unearthed now and revealed in their true colours. They were just valueless junk and not worth the expense of storing. A great bonfire was lit in the orchard and the mountain of garbage was gradually burnt over a period of days. There was no convenient tip or dump to take it to, and no skips to be hired then. Consumption by fire was the only solution.

Inside the house I was packing trunks and suitcases and filling tea chests and packing cases with small things like books, ornaments, china and glass etc. The removal men would only have to deal with the furniture, carpets and pictures.

"You do realise you will have to scrub every floor and clean all the paintwork after the furniture has been removed, don't you?" enquired a helpful friend - although she was not feeling helpful enough to volunteer to assist.

No, I had not realised this horrifying fact. I had never had to vacate a house before in my eight years of married life.

Well, the dear, much-treasured Mrs. Owen and I would have to manage this mammoth task between us. One of us could scrub all the old oak floors upstairs. The other would have to cope with downstairs, which included huge flagstones in the kitchen, scullery, hall, larder and dairy.

The removal men marched in and out loading our possessions into their vast van.

The patches of wall, round which I had had to paint when a piece of furniture was too massive for me to move unaided, were now exposed for all to see. The carpetless floors were deep in dust, especially in the hall, where the flagstones had been covered for years with thick, but permeable, rush matting. It was all rather shame-making.

After many hours of first brushing and then scrubbing and rinsing floors, involving much carrying of heavy buckets of water, I felt as limp and useless as a pricked balloon. But the farmhouse had never before looked so clean. No-one had performed this last duty for us, prior to our moving in.

The furniture remover's pantechnicon had departed, taking our furniture to be stored in Hereford until we found another farm. The car waited outside, full of suitcases, and our two wardrobe trunks completely filled the attached pig-trailer.

After changing my filthy outer clothes in the now spotlessly clean kitchen, I crammed them into a large bag to be thrown onto the seemingly eternal flames of the bonfire. The kitchen looked unnaturally immaculate. You could eat off the floor now, but it no longer looked like home. The Insulted Crag was cold and lifeless. The telephone, marooned in the middle of the floor, was silent. All the windows and doors were shut and bolted, and the remaining squad of six or seven cats locked out from their haven of warmth and food. Soon, I hoped, the new owners of Caldicott would arrive, rescue the cats, feed and stroke them. Then they would light the stove and bring the old house alive again.

We locked the back door for the last time. The key was to be left in the dependable hands of Mrs. Thomas the Post.

As I got out of the car to open the gate onto the road I met Cookapoo, who was returning from a hunting expedition. He was a member of the cat 'care and maintenance party'.

"Goodbye dear old Cookapoo," I said in a choked voice and, as an afterthought, "Heil Hitler!"

He raised his right front leg in a final salute. I shut the gate carefully, then jumped into the car and we drove away. I did not dare look back.

192

Twenty-Eight
Fresh Fields

Some months before, we had promised ourselves a treat. When we finally left Caldicott, we would stay in a luxury country hotel, just a few miles away, for a short time. So after saying a sad goodbye to Broad Oak, we arrived at our rather grand hotel, with the pig-trailer, now unnaturally clean and containing our two large trunks, linked to the back of the car.

By this time my charwoman's knees were buckling under me, so I made straight for the large, comfortable bedroom and went to bed. Never mind if it was only 5 p.m. in the afternoon; I was too tired to eat anything, do anything, or even think. For a few days we wallowed in the twin luxuries of wonderful food and being waited on hand and foot, and were able to recharge our flat batteries. It was money well spent.

After our recuperative break, we felt strong enough to cope with Chinkie's inevitable questions and comments, and drove across England to her house in Bury St. Edmunds. This was to be our home base while we searched for our next farm.

Chinkie had lived in Bury St. Edmunds for the previous thirty years or so, constantly buying and then selling her houses. At that time she and Margaret were occupying a three-storey house with a basement. As usual, the house was extremely cold. It had been built in the days of servants and blazing fires in every room. Now the enormous sitting room, so beautifully furnished with antiques, was only faintly heated by a small, old-fashioned, spluttering gas fire: the kind that scorched your feet and ankles when you sat close to it, but left the rest of the body cold. Most day-to-day living happened on the ground floor and on the first floor, where Chinkie, Margaret and Helen all had their own bedrooms. There were two attic bedrooms and a boxroom above, previously occupied by servants. Harry and I found ourselves directed up the attic stairs. These were uncarpeted, as the last vestiges of comfort and civilisation disappeared after the first floor. Our bedroom had some furniture, but at the time no actual bed, just two mattresses on the floor. The basement was also beyond the pale. More uncarpeted stairs led down to a damp, unheated kitchen and even colder scullery. But there was one cosy little room, next to the kitchen, probably the old servants' hall. This was used as a dining room. In the passage outside the kitchen was a food lift which would transport trays of food etc., first up to, then down from, the ground floor. It was operated by turning a handle.

From this house we planned our strategy. "Where shall we start looking?" had to be the first question. "How much can we afford to spend?" the second. Although neither of us had ever been there, we mutually decided we did not like the Midlands. The North East would be too cold, the North West too wet. East Anglia, as we knew well, had heavy, stick-to-the-boots soil, and Harry did not want to return to the land of his fathers and farm in Wales. That left the south of England from Kent to Cornwall.

Particulars of farms for sale in Kent, Surrey, Sussex, Hampshire, Wiltshire, Dorset, Somerset, Devon and Cornwall were sent for, and sheaves of large, heavy envelopes addressed to us plummeted through the letter-box. As expected, any suitably sized dairy farms in Kent, Surrey and Sussex etc. were far too high-priced. "I expect we shall end up in Somerset, Devon or Cornwall," Harry predicted. All the same we decided to have a look at the most hopeful sounding farms in every county, regardless of price. It would be educational.

Determined to do our farm hunting in a thoroughly business-like way, we devised a system of points for each farm inspected. So many points for price, house, buildings, land, position, services available, distance from towns, and so on. At the end of our quest, when we had investigated all the farms on our list, we would add up the points and see who was the winner.

Armed with our list of 'possibles', we started our search in Kent. I fell in love immediately with the first farm we saw, although it would be more accurate to say with the first farmhouse. It was an old Kentish building: the oasthouse at one end had been converted to human habitation and incorporated in the farmhouse. Round houses had always fascinated me, although I did realise how difficult it must be to fit rectangular furniture into circular rooms.

"This is *it!*" I told Harry. "When looking for something you always either find it straight away or at the very end. We needn't look any further. I've always wanted to live in an oasthouse."

"Yes, it is a lovely house, but you must be more realistic," Harry reminded me. "The farmhouse is the least important part of a farm, the land and buildings come first, and anyhow, we can't afford it."

We moved on to Surrey and Sussex, where the situation was the same. Inevitably, so near to London, all farms were beyond our pocket. Farms were inspected by us during daylight hours and then we would make for the nearest town and select some small, comfortable hotel for the night, usually a Trust House. Bed and breakfast and evening meal did not cost an arm and a leg in the 1950's, and we could afford to rest comfortably after an energetic day walking round at least two farms. Hampshire, Dorset and Wiltshire yielded no possibilities either, but we began to strike oil, as Harry had predicted, when we reached the West Country. In the less fashionable parts we started to find farms at our price; places that already had mains electricity. Many of them in North Somerset seemed to incorporate the word 'Huish' in their name. We walked round Huish this and Huish that and Something Huish too. It was an odd word, pronounced, apparently, like a sneeze. I wondered what

Huish meant, and decided it was probably a local word for 'hairy'; most of those farms came into this category.

We discovered that Devon is a huge county and it took a long time to do our researching there, even though we ignored Dartmoor and the surrounding district: too much dense fog, too many escaped convicts and 'Hounds of the Baskervilles'. The South Hams sounded just right for a dairy farm, and it was: a lovely fertile area and appropriately expensive. It was December when we made our inspection of Devon and heavy snow fell while we were staying in Tavistock. The trusty old green and red Vauxhall found it could not climb the snow-covered hill out of Tavistock, and we had to return to the town to have snow chains fitted to the tyres.

Then we crossed the Tamar, left England behind and entered a foreign land. Most Cornish farms are small and more like smallholdings. A hundred-acre farm in Cornwall is considered large. We scoured the Duchy from end to end. There seemed to be plenty of farms in this far-away country at our price. North Cornwall appeared much more windswept than the south, even though the two coasts are so close together. Along the north coast all the little stunted trees and bushes were growing at an angle of sixty degrees, cringing away from the Atlantic gales. At Wadebridge we met the auctioneers Button, Menhennit and Mutton for the first time. We could not possibly forget a name like that, and noted with equal amusement that the chief corn merchants in Truro were called Hoskin, Trevithick and Polkinhorn.

One Cornish farm will be forever engraved in my mind. This one was near Helston in the south of the county. On paper it sounded almost ideal, although there was no photograph. However, right at the end of the description of the house there were two surprising statements. One said: "Unfortunately it has a tin roof." The other announced: "Water is by rain." You cannot get more basic than that.

Was it a coincidence that it was raining hard when we arrived in Helston that morning? A kind of cloudburst was descending on the little town famous for its Floral Dance, when Harry stopped the car outside the main hotel where we intended to stay that night. Helston was obviously organised to deal with torrents of rain, although we did not know this until it was too late. At the base of each kerb, instead of the usual shallow gutter there was a deep channel to drain away surplus water. It was raining much too hard to see this so Harry drove up to the kerb and thence into the hidden drain. The car tipped up sideways, I found myself sliding down to the left, while Harry, still at the wheel, was sitting above me on the right.

Immediately, even before we could guess what had happened, two chaps from the garage next to the hotel, rushed out with ropes and strong wooden beams. "Stay there!" they shouted, even though we had no other option, "We'll have you out directly." Rope was passed round the car and two planks placed underneath. "Heave ho!" one of them cried, and the car was levered into the air and pulled back onto the road again.

"Well, thank you very much," Harry said to our saviours, realising that they must make a good living out of the drainage channels and their primitive rescue apparatus. "How much do I owe you?" They named a pretty hefty sum of money as the going rate, but we were in no position to argue about it.

That afternoon we drove out to the farm with the unfortunate tin roof. The deluge continued and the farmer did not greet us very effusively. "'Tis no weather to go walking round them there fields," he said, "but you could look at the house and buildings I s'pose." As we explored the dark rooms of the farmhouse in the gloom of a wet December afternoon, we could hear the rain drumming on the tin roof. That noise lost the farm many points. It would be impossible to sleep at night with such a racket overhead.

197

Next, enshrouded in waterproof coats, hats and boots, we walked round the buildings. In the centre of the farmyard was an enormous midden, many times the size of the one at Caldicott. The surrounding path was narrow and slippery, and the midden itself, owing to all the rain, now more like a black, evil-smelling lake. No wonder the particulars had said "water by rain": it seemed perfectly feasible now.

It was not Harry's day. He slipped on the greasy surface of the path and plunged into the midden. When he emerged everything he wore, right down to his skin, was soaked in stinking liquid manure. "Oh my dear life!" exclaimed the farmer. "You don't belong to fall in *there*. Better go 'ome and change your clothes before you catch your death." He did not offer to rub Harry down or lend him some dry clothes, but was just anxious to get us off his premises as quickly as possible. I asked for some newspaper and we spread it on the driver's seat. Harry drove back to Helston shivering and with chattering teeth. Torrents of rain were still falling when we drew up, carefully avoiding the gushing gutter, outside a shop in the main street which said: 'Gentlemen's Outfitters' and underneath: 'Everything Supplied'.

I do not know how we mustered the courage to go in but we were desperate, and a desperate situation requires desperate measures. The shop owner and his two young, male assistants blenched when they saw and smelt Harry.

"I want a complete change of clothing," Harry said. "Coat, hat, jacket, pullover, shirt, trousers, vest, pants, socks and shoes."

"Come this way sir," the owner said, ushering him into a cubicle, and, to his assistant, "Go and get lots of newspaper, boy."

I stayed outside and watched while Harry divested himself of all his clothes, which he flung through the cubicle curtains into a malodorous heap on the pile of newspapers laid on the floor of the shop. He was handed a dressing gown.

"Now sir," said the gentlemen's outfitter, "if you will follow me, I'll take you to where you can have a wash." Three quarters of an hour later, much cleaner, but also very much poorer, Harry and I left the shop. From head to toe everything he wore was brand, spanking new, right down to the clean handkerchief in his pocket.

"Would you like us to try to have your clothes cleaned?" asked the shop owner rather hopelessly.

"No thank you. Throw them away please," Harry replied.

After we had reached Land's End there was no more land left for us to inspect, so we stopped at a little hotel for a few days to rest and do our sums. The points earned by each farm we had walked over were added up, and we now knew the winner. It was sixty-six-acre Trudgeons Farm, at Sticker, near St. Austell, on the south coast. We had been amused by the name when we first read the particulars of this farm. Added to the address it sounded as if everyone farming there would have to get used to taking plenty of exercise, in glutinous ground. But now we decided we would be the ones who got stuck there.

Trudgeons had a great deal going for it. First, the price was right; the house adequate, with a bathroom etc., and mains electricity already installed; the farm buildings were less elderly than those at Caldicott, and there were two modern Dutch barns, as well as a new Danish piggery. Once again part of the land lay on a hill, although this time the house was at the bottom of the hill and actually in the village of Sticker. So there were two shops, a pub, a garage, buses and even a once-a-week fish and chip shop, conveniently at hand. It was two and a half miles from St. Austell and three miles from the sea.

After making an offer for the farm, which was accepted, we were told we would get possession three months later in March. Much relieved that our hunt had been successful, we returned to Bury St. Edmunds to spend Christmas with Chinkie, Margaret and Helen.

Front of Trudgeons farmhouse

Cows at Trudgeons

Before we left Cornwall, we decided to return in January. We had three months to spare and this would give us time to get to know the district, towns and countryside, and perhaps some of the local people, before moving into Trudgeons. So we made arrangements to stay with another farming family.

As we made the long journey back to Suffolk we reflected on what we had now let ourselves in for. This farm was going to be a much harder taskmistress than Caldicott. We had sentenced ourselves to three hundred and sixty-five days a year of twice-daily milking, but it still seemed a sensible decision. We hoped it would take us up a few more rungs on the 'farming ladder'.

Margaret and I were jointly in charge of preparations for the Christmas dinner, so spent many extra hours down in the basement kitchen that Christmas. She was 'Mrs. Bridges' and I played the part of 'Ivy' the kitchen maid. There was no turkey, either high or low, arriving by train from Caldicott that year, so a massive bird had been bought from the poulterers. It was almost too large for the conventional-sized gas oven, but this fact had its bright side. It meant the turkey had to start cooking early in the morning and the normally cold kitchen actually became warm. A little heat percolated through to the scullery where 'Ivy' peeled potatoes and prepared all the vegetables. Then we created lots of hot steam with numerous pans of boiling water crammed together on the top of the cooker. Margaret was determined the turkey should have every single trimming available.

After Christmas came the usual seasonal lull when all the shops were shut for a few days and doctors and dentists had disappeared mysteriously into thin air. A period of endless cold turkey when even the most sweet-toothed had become satiated with chocolates, Christmas cake, pudding and mince pies and fancied only the tangerines. During this time of limbo somebody urgently needed medicine or pills. We consulted the local paper for emergency chemists, and found Boots would be open for an hour between midday and 1 p.m. The whole party went on the expedition to the chemist, just to get some exercise and a change of scene. Only the pharmacy was open, all the rest of the shop was still firmly shut, including the lending library. Chinkie's eyes lit up when she saw the library again, even though a large prominent notice said: 'Library Closed until Dec. 28th'. A low velvet rope had been artistically looped around the library limits to deter people from walking in and browsing among the books. Carefully unhooking the rope barrier with the tip of her silver-topped stick, Chinkie walked in and started looking through the shelves.

"Mummy!" whispered Helen, as loudly as she dared. "The library is shut."

"Yes dear, but they don't mean me," replied Chinkie.

Never mind, tomorrow she would be able to visit the library quite legally, and we would be heading for Cornwall, and who knows what new experiences.

Epilogue

Well, I have told you as much as I can remember of my early memories and, looking back, I am very, very glad about all the things I was able to do. I was lucky to have experiences that most people did not have, and I enjoyed my life very much, especially the part when I was married to Harry, and we were both able to do what we liked, which was to live in the country, have animals, and really not have too many financial worries.

On the whole I have been very happy: I think I am by nature more inclined to be happy than unhappy, and I am delighted with the life that I have been given. Thank you, God!

By the same author: MAKING THE MOST OF IT

Sonia Tudor was born during the First World War into a world that has long since vanished - of Norland Nannies, butlers and debutantes.

This privileged and happy early life ended abruptly with the separation of her parents. She and her brother found themselves attending an ever-changing series of boarding schools and having no fixed abode.

Not long after leaving school the Second World War broke out, and she joined the WAAF. She served abroad in Egypt, Italy and Algeria as a Code and Cypher Officer until 1945.

Making The Most Of It recounts the adventures and exploits of both a schoolgirl and a WAAF Officer always keen to see how life can be lived at its fullest.